A CHROI

OF

EMOTIVE
TALES

The rite of passage

By

JOHN JT ROBERTS

MENS SANA IN COPORE SANO
(A healthy mind in a healthy body)

Published by John JT Roberts

First printing in April 2019

Copyright © 2019 John JT Roberts

Twitter: @johnjrj348

www. facebook.com/jrj348

Printed in the United Kingdom and the U.S.A.

ISBN-9798643226499

Cover designed and prepared by the author

CONTENTS

DEDICATION

FOREWORD

THE KEY

THE SEQUENCE OF TALES:

--

DEDICATED

TO

Friends, colleagues, and all fellow servicemen, who have experienced the distress of active service. To Brothers and Sisters lost, injured or ill, while serving throughout the world.

WE SHALL REMEMBER THEM

THE RITE OF PASSAGE

FOREWORD

This book intends to encourage the reader to reflect on their journey, from childhood to adulthood. Inevitably, there would have been experiences in your life which have led to the present **'YOU'**!

Did such occasions along the pathway of life, contribute to the extraordinary person you have become?

There is no doubt, that each one of us is, without exception, extraordinary!

We all have traits, aptitudes, and constraints, which we were born with that cannot be explained in simple terms. However, everyone has a certain assemblage of qualities that are transposed into the building blocks of one's character. These can have an adverse or beneficial effect on the individual and can lead to the way one is perceived by others. Many individuals are powerful and strong, whilst others are prone to less vigorous lifestyles. Some are fortunate enough to have a greater mix of characteristics that result in outstanding physical and mental ability. Often (as I have witnessed) a physically active and healthy lifestyle contributes to an improvement in mental aptitude.

These stories are not in any specific order or about any topic. But they are intended to lead the reader to the conclusion that one's experience contributes to the 'Person'! I hope readers of this book find it sufficiently motivational, emotionally justifiable to warrant the use of their valuable time. The diversity of themes and topics suggest that what is to the individual a mundane and pointless recollection, can be for others be an interesting and poignant reflection of their own experiences.

The tales are designed to inspire others to reflect on their own extraordinary lives. I hope to encourage them to tell us all about themselves through the satisfying medium known as 'The Written Word'. If this does happen, even in one case, then I would consider it a rewarding result and a successful outcome. There is but one life, make the most of it and excite us with tales of your life's experiences.

JT

THE KEY

The images below are used to emphasise the emotive sequence.

INSPIRATION

The Welsh Dragon

Always of immense inspirational value to all Welsh people, especially when experiencing, conflict, oppression, or fear.

COMPASSION

The Dog

Mans best friend and reliable companion. Ever faithful, courageous, and loyal. An animal favoured in communities throughout the world.

TREPIDATION

The hands of friendship

The bringing together of people having been separated, incarcerated by circumstance, degradation, conflict, and war

----

INTRIGUE

The mystic East. An intriguing place with strange customs, beautiful cultures, and monuments. To go there adds great value to one's life experience.

ERUDITION

A meaningful term for people who are prepared to research, study, and learn. A scholarly, literate well-read individual who has a pragmatic approach to education.

COURAGE

This is a test of mettle, nerve, and indomitable spirit. Usually under threat of injury or death to the individual. Chickens are normally thought to lack courage!

FEAR

Broadly speaking, snakes, spiders and ghosts are thought to be prominent instigators of fear. Fear can manifest itself in many ways, but in this case, the Grimm Reaper highlights the intense feeling of impending doom.

RITE OF PASSAGE

Passing a test or passing some sort of physical challenge, to become a member of a special group or organisation. To be culturally and morally acceptable to others involved.

1

INSPIRATION

CYMRU AM BYTH

Welsh dragon

A TALE FROM THE VALLEY'S

(Wales 1940s)

PENYRHEDYN

(Village above the ferns)

This is a story about a young disabled Welsh boy, who lived in a beautifully dappled stone cottage in the tiny mountain village of Penyrhedyn. The village is located above the dense fern lines on a mountainside in South Wales. The cottage stands beside a steep narrow mountain road, at the high end of the village. It has large gardens with fruit trees, vegetables, and flowers. A sloping roof to one side of the building' stretching from the top floor, to within a foot of the ground. Sliding down the roof from the top window became a regular pastime for the boy and his twin sister Anita. At about a foot thick, the roof was built by the boys'

father as a defence against stray wartime bombs.

There was no electricity or running water during his childhood, so they used an outside loo which lay concealed among the trees at the top of the garden. His duties included collecting water from a stream several hundred yards higher up the mountain. His older brothers and sisters had been responsible for doing this job for many years, but now it was his turn to fetch and carry. It helped to develop his strength and made him more independent.

He loved to go up to the stream outflow pipe because the Italian POW's often worked in the fields just alongside the mountain path. They sang Italian love songs as they worked and waved to him as he waited to fill his water cans. Sometimes they gave him fantastic toys they had made from old wood and slate. They even gave him paintings and drawings to take home for his mam and dad. It was a happy time for him, his twin sister, and the whole family.

Across the field at the back of the cottage, a narrow path passed an old coal mine hidden by trees and bushes. The entrance was dark, damp and foreboding, with tree roots hanging over its entrance just like spider's webs. Nobody dared go there alone because it was miserable and haunted! Alongside the mine shaft, a tall unused chimney stack sang in the wind, just like a big trombone. It was high, impossible to climb and topped by a crown of thick foliage. Seen from the valley below the stack became a symbol of the past mining heritage of the region! Further along the path, a pine forest ran along the slopes, where springy pine needles carpeted the ground. Red squirrels, foxes and other animals lived and wandered among the tall scented trees. It was a great place for children to play, but a long way from home. It was worth it, but whenever his mam blew her silver referees whistle it meant 'get back home' or else?

The boy's dad was a coal miner and a keen gardener, builder, and boxer. He used to fight for Barnham's Circus, whenever it came to Wales, and never lost a fight in five years. But above all, he was renowned for his calm and friendly disposition.

One day the lad asked his dad a question about why the Red Dragon was on the Welsh flag. His dad told him it was is a symbol that showed they were courageous people and that it was the oldest National flag in the world. The boy wanted to know if the Red Dragon was real or just pretend? His dad eventually convinced him it was real, otherwise, it would not have been on the Welsh flag. His dad then asked him why he asked so many questions about the dragon? The young boy told him he'd seen a Red Dragon at the mountain-top two days earlier.

This worried his dad because the boy was born with weak legs and wore callipers to help him walk. He was told to be careful when he walked up to the top and made to promise he would take extra care whenever he went up there. Anyway, his Dad did not mind because it was good exercise and helped the lad get even stronger. So, he agreed to let him go up there, providing he told somebody before leaving. The boy wondered if the Red Dragon was lonely living up there on his own, perhaps he wanted company? Over the next few weeks, he struggled to the top and sat for hours above the quarry, hoping to meet The Great Welsh Dragon. He sang his favourite Welsh songs, shouted, and whistled as hard as possible to get the Red Dragon to appear. When nothing happened, he seemed so sad and disappointed his dad decided to tell him a tale he heard from an old villager many years earlier.

When rounding up ewes and lambs on the mountain, Old Danny Watts, who owned the little village shop (community centre) had told him that he had seen a dragon-like creature sitting above the mountain-top quarry. At the time, Danny felt the wind drop and the air becomes still. The lambs huddled into their mothers as if they were afraid of something. Old Danny was so scared he dared not go up there ever again. According to his dad, nobody had ever seen anything like it or even heard anything about it, before or since.

The boy thought to himself "if the Red Dragon is on the Welsh flag it can't be bad!".

Dad told him old Danny was scared because the dragon-like creature vanished in a puff of smoke. The boy wondered how that could be possible until his dad told him about the legend of the ferns. Before beginning his story, his dad asked if he ever sat on the mountain-top and seen things disappear into a haze, even on a bright day. The boy remembered seeing this happen but had never mentioned it. Dad went on to explain that fern pollen spores could often hide things because there were so many of them during the spore season. Sometimes, there were so many they could even hide the village houses from anyone looking down from the mountains, or up from the valleys. The very next day, even before his breakfast, the boy made his way to his special spot on the mountain top. He sat for ages looking out for any signs of spores and the same for several days, but nothing happened.

Then one bright, sunny morning, as he approached the mountain gate, he heard a frightened lamb crying out for its mother. He hurried towards the sound, to discover the lamb sinking into one of the bog holes on the mountainside. Its mother was running around frantically bleating as if crying for help. He had seen his dad rescue lambs from these dangerous bog holes several times and knew what to do. Collecting a huge bundle of reeds, he laid them from the edge of the bog hole towards the centre. They were long and strong enough for him to lie on, to reach the struggling lamb. Grabbing the lamb by the ears, he pulled until the lamb came out with a great big plop covered in mud and slime. The lamb shook itself and wiggled its tail before running to its mam for comfort, before running off as fast as they could go.

By the time he reached the mountain-top, the boy felt tired and needed a rest. He was so tired he nearly fell over the edge of the quarry, but a strong gust of wind seemed to help him recover his balance. It was getting late and the ferns waved in the wind beside him. He felt chilly then everything suddenly became still and it got warmer. It was as if an invisible blanket had been placed around him. Moments later something began to shimmer just beside him, his eyes got wider and he began to tremble with fear.

As he watched a strange reddish shape appeared, it was the 'Great Red Welsh Dragon'. The dragon smiled and sat down beside him and made himself comfortable. The boy could barely breathe but stopped himself from running home and hiding in the bomb-shelter coal shed.

The Red dragon sat cross-legged looking out over the valleys, before commenting (in a deep 'sing-song' voice) about the wonderful view. He even called the boy by his name, which made the lad wonder how that was possible. The Red dragon explained that he often sat beside him when he was at the top and told him not to worry. He went on to mutter a few words in Welsh, then said how much he admired him for being so brave when saving the lamb. But! the Red dragon told him he did not care for his whistling very much because it hurt his ears. Then he warned him to be careful at the quarry top because it was extremely dangerous. The boy then realised it could have been the Red Dragon, not the wind, that had saved him from falling over the edge of the quarry a few days earlier.

As he grew in confidence, he asked the Red dragon why he lived on the mountaintop all alone. The Red dragon told him he had lots of great friends around the countryside. The animals in the fields and other creatures living on and around the mountain. He and one of his best friends, Major the Carthorse, often enjoyed galloping around the fields together. Puzzled, the boy asked the Red dragon how he kept hidden when he flew around the countryside?

"It's to do with the fern spores, which can make you invisible" explained the Red Dragon. 'They can be made into wonderful cloaks that you can hide under when you don't want to be seen".

The dragon went on to tell him how he collected the spores each time they spawned, and how he stored them in his cosy den down below in the quarry.

"By heck, the story dad told me earlier about the fern cloaks was true after all" shouted the boy.

The Red dragon told him he and his friends had decided they should reward him for bravery when saving the lamb. They all thought it a good idea for the Red dragon to take him along on some of his travels. The boy was thrilled but sat and pondered for a while, before telling the Red dragon his mam would be furious if he went off for a long time without telling her. She would be hopping mad and even angrier if he did not go home when the whistle sounded. This made the Red dragon smile before explaining, that time stood still for ordinary folk under the fern cloak. This meant they could go anywhere they wanted and be back before being missed by anyone.

"fantastic" shouted the lad calling the Red dragon Sir when he thanked him.

That is when the Red dragon told him his name was Dafydd, not Sir! The boy was so pleased he asked if he could go on a trip with Dafydd the very same day. Dafydd scratched his head, before saying they could go on a quick visit to Mount Snowdon, the highest most beautiful mountain in Wales. Thrilled to bits, the boy said he hoped they could go before his mam blew her silver referees whistle!

Shortly after, Dafydd suggested the youngster should sit between his wings and hold on to his short horns. Then he pulled a fluffy fern cloak from a pouch near his belt and tossed it over them both. A great calm came over the boy as they flew to the most impressive mountain in all of Wales, where the views were even better than they were in Penyrhedyn. Dafydd told him there were many wonderful places around the world and that one day they would visit them together. The boy felt as though the entire world was his playground and hugged the Great Welsh Dragon. The dragon knew the boy's mam and dad were proud of the youngster because he was good, thoughtful, and brave. But now they must make their way back home. When they arrived home the boy thanked Dafydd for an incredible adventure.

Suddenly, the shrill sound of a referee's whistle came from the lone cottage far below. It was mam calling! So, with a wave of his hand, he headed for home as fast as he could go. The smell of freshly baked bread encouraged him to move even faster. Dafydd smiled as the boy hurried away, convinced the lad was getting stronger with each passing day. Then he too slowly disappeared. Over the next few months, the boy told nobody about his new best friend Dafydd and their adventures in faraway places, or about meeting so many other dragons.

Many Dragons lived on islands, others lived in mountains and other strange places. There were Red dragons, Green dragons, Blue dragons, and even Yellow dragons. Although he saw many exciting places, he still loved it when he and his friend Dafydd just sat looking out over the valleys and chatting together. It was such an exciting time for the disabled Welsh boy from the village above the ferns.

He kept a record of everything that happened in a secret notebook which he hid under his bed. And often wondered if he should tell his dad about his incredible adventures with Dafydd.

Now, 70+ years later he understood why it had not been necessary, his dad would have known all about it, anyway! Dad had planted the seeds of adventure and love of life into the mind of the boy, along with the fighting spirit of Welshness. Looked over by his alter-ego, Dafydd. It would not be an exaggeration to say that several incidents occurred throughout his life, which was connected to dragons in one way or another. Such as the fantastic Komodo dragons of far-off Indonesia, or the mystical island of Pulau Tioman (dragon island) in the South China Sea.

Because of his chores, fetching and carrying water in larger and larger cans in his early years, his strength and fitness developed. This led to his adventures up hills and mountains in many countries of the world. His legs were now so strong he no longer needed callipers and had grown up to become a super fit soldier. His undiminished power of imagination, strength of character, belief in himself and his subconscious alter-ego, remains with him to this day.

END

DAFYDD

I know this to be true, for I am That Boy.

"Oh, just a minute, I thought I heard a referees whistle'! You must excuse me I have to dash!"

INSPIRATION

Have you been inspired by the above reflective tale of youth, adventure, and dreams? Is there a correlation between past events and your life at present? Does it make you contemplate the possibility that myths, legends, and dreams, have contributed to your life in a positive beneficial way?

If so, this story reflecting on childhood has been a success. It could initiate a response, that encourages you to write about your childhood, and how it affected your future life, generally!

It is my sincere hope that it does.
Pleasant dreams.

DEDICATED TO MY
DEAR PARENTS

DRAGONS

Of course, there are dragons
Those myths and legends abound
But only when you take the time
Can any of them be found?

2

COMPASSION

NORTH BORNEO

MOUNT KINABALU
4,095.2 metres

(13,435 feet)

THE COMPASSIONATE

SOLDIER
(Borneo Circa 1960)

'Ghosts, Cam-cream and Maggots'

In all his years of active service and military training JT had never felt as vulnerable as he did when the patrol stumbled upon a pitiful sight, whilst patrolling in the jungle-covered mountains of Borneo. What had been silent, hostile, and difficult world of the past few days, had changed into a nauseating soul-destroying hell? Concealed beside the path in the shadowy fringe of dense undergrowth, the patrol stood silently and saw a scene of sickening horror. A pack of about eight feral dogs appeared from out of the bush and mustered on a wide section of track. What materialised before them shocked even the strongest combat experienced men amongst them.

As a patrol leader, JT gathered his composure and realising that it was just a matter of time before the pack saw the patrol. A vice-like agony enveloped his heart, as he struggled to control the trembling and disgust at the scene before him. The distress was reflected on the faces of his companions, accompanied by muffled mutterings of anger and despair. The reality of what happened was brought into focus when a single voice expressed the feelings of all present.

"My God boss, we must do something!"

JT had to accept responsibility for any action that was undertaken. His priority had to be the safety of the men, and his duties as a combat soldier. His emotions had to be suppressed, even though the situation was inhumane. The need for support was paramount in his decision to wait, this came from his friend and second-in-command Sgt Jock the Highlander.

"Ye canna do a thing JT, but it's dam hard".

JT had to decide what could or should be done, to sort out the dreadful sight laid out before them. The scene changed dramatically; when screams shattered the silence, of the majestic jungle-clad hills that surrounded them. Screeching birds and howling monkeys added their voices to the milieu before the echoes fell into precipitous damp valleys. The deathly silence that followed, made the place darker and even more depressing.

For a couple of hours before this incident, the patrol had enjoyed the relative comfort of an easy-going mountain trail. Before that, they had experienced three days, that could only be described as a rapid weight-loss programme. Plodding through thick skin scarring thorn, ankle-deep in decaying mush and sweltering humidity. The leach and snake-infested shadows made worse by steep, damp, slippery slopes.

It seemed like a lifetime since they had arrived at the small fishing village, beside the Tempasuk river. Dawn was about to break, as the seven-man inflatable was unloaded and hidden among the reeds. Seven ghostly figures melted into the shadows of the jungle canopy, leaving no sign to show they had ever been there. From that point on talking was kept to an absolute minimum, there could be no smoking, cooking or latrine digging. Desperation toilet facilities were provided by way of plastic bags, which were sealed and kept in the individual's pack. To be disposed of when they arrived at a suitable location, or back at base camp.

Sounds and smells discouraged, individuals were camouflaged with twigs, leaves and cam-creamed faces. Instructions were by way of hand, eye, and body movements. This was a deadly place, where mistakes could lead to serious injury or death. These men had trained and worked together as a team for months. Perfecting their skills and developing their fitness and stamina, to withstand the harsh jungle environment.

Their mission was to familiarise themselves with the area surrounding the strategic airfield, which lay on the plain below Mount Kinabalu. It was great training and preparation, for the confrontation between the regional powers of Malaysia and Indonesia. The exercise promoted knowledge, experience, and confidence, which would be invaluable should they be called upon to counter enemy groups infiltrating the region?

Fortunately (or unfortunately, depending on one's point of view) this was the last day of a four-day jungle training exercise. It had been a difficult start trudging through razor-sharp thorn patches, bamboo thickets and leach infested undergrowth. Poisonous snakes, lizards and all manner of dangerous insects, plants and animals existed in the hot and humid environment. It was essential for each member of the team to develop an understanding of the dangers, and how best to avoid them. 'Carelessness kills and tiredness is no excuse!' was the premise upon which the training was based?

Cam cream, mud, twigs, and foliage of all descriptions were essential ingredients for concealment. These offered scant protection against mosquitoes, hornets, and other beasties. Regular checks for leeches was carried out before the offending bloodsuckers (there were many) were removed with a flick of the wrist. Insect repellent was used sparingly because the result of contact with eyes or private parts was agonizing. Yet, there were the occasional moral boosting moments, such as farting, quiet comments about wives, girlfriends, or both. Besides, frequent announcements from Jock, that everyone hated!

"Och! I wish I were in the heelands, with a wee dram and a fair lassie".

Decisions on what food should be taken were up to individual members of the patrol. Wrong choices could cause low energy levels, poor fluid retention or other serious health problems. Experienced members offered advice, but individuals had to decide according to personal preference. Tins of food could not be taken, for obvious reasons, such as smell, sound, weight, and disposal. Chocolate, rice balls, dried fruit and vegetables were popular. Food wrappings were lightweight and kept to a minimum, with each man carrying at least two rubber topped water bottles.

A radio unit was held in reserve for serious accidents or emergencies. If activated, a signal of the exact location of the patrol was sent to the operations room back at base camp. A response team would then mount a rescue mission. Unless an incident constituted an emergency or the patrol was in serious imminent danger, the signal would not be sent. Accidents were a regular feature of training, in this environment. These were dealt with by one specialist medic within the group, known as Doc. Doc, was one of the most proficient, able, and likeable characters in the group, besides being one of the ugliest!

On this training exercise, there had been minor injuries from thorns, insect bites and bamboo slivers. Jungle ulcers, prickly heat, skin tinea were common complaints. There had been no serious accidents during the past three, long labour-intensive days. Progress had been slow, nights were cold, damp, and miserable. Sleep was virtually impossible, apart from catnaps. Even midway up Mount Kinabalu, there were low-lying swampy areas, infested with many nasty inhabitants that were best avoided. For first timers within the group, this was an experience they would often reflect upon with pride in clubs, pubs and at reunions. Yet it was not all doom and gloom, as several amusing, but difficult incidents proved. These were positive antidotes for the misery inflicted by the unforgiving terrain.

On one occasion the patrol lay hidden in dense undergrowth, bitten and scratched in stinking mud for almost two hours. Before realising that the persons, who appeared to be observing them, were not human's but Orangutans. The patrol leader (JT) was at the receiving end of many silent, meaningful hand gestures and jibes as a result. But he was confident it had been a good opportunity to test the mettle of the patrol members, and himself.

Another incident bordered on a dangerous, yet humorous event, which could have led to disastrous consequences. The patrol had followed an animal track through a damp, thorn, and bamboo laden area for several hundred yards. Because the going was so difficult, it was impossible to go ahead at a reasonable pace or to avoid dangerous delays. Eventually emerging from the brutal tangled undergrowth, they discovered a track meandering through the forest, like a river of hope. The track was one of many permanent highways, used by large forest animals (Elephant, Water buffalo and the like).

They followed the track for some time before they entered an open clearing. The ground was damp and boggy, which reminded him of the bog holes he had encountered as a young boy. Fortunately, it was clear of undergrowth, which allowed them to enjoy some sunlight and open sky. After a short break, the order was given to move on. Just as the patrol cleared the bog, they became aware of desperate curses coming from the clearing. The response was rapid and the laughter quietly hilarious, especially when they heard the Doc muttering, in *'The French vernacular'*.

"My f*****g leg is stuck in this muddy, foul-smelling, stinking hole".

"You're stuck in an Elephants leg-hole, you daft sod", commented Jock.

Followed by the usual "Och! I wish I were in the heelands with a wee dram and a fair lassie".

"Bollocks, you Scots git, get me out of here" Screamed the swamp monster.

"You were told you not to step in any puddles or areas that looked wet" added the amused JT.

What had the appearance of a simple little puddle, was where an elephant's leg had sunk to at least 4ft in the muck. This created an incredibly powerful suction. The unfortunate *Ugly Dock-ling* was stuck up to his crutch, unable to move without becoming more and more imprisoned. A harness was improvised and placed around the unfortunate man's shoulders, he was unceremoniously dragged out of the offending hole, kicking and cursing. There was a huge uniformed gurgle in response, as the oozy suction released its grip. The smell, left by the animal faeces and urine mix, in the muddy hollow, was horrendous. Which meant that the unfortunate Doc was sent to *Coventry and* kept at a respectable distance for some time after. Everyone hoped that they would not need his services for a while! On a more serious note, it had reinforced the

importance of being careful in this
incredibly dangerous place.

On day two, the patrol stopped for a rest
in a small clearing. There was a strange
unusual smell in the air, which was worth
investigating. They cautiously worked the
surrounding jungle, knowing it was more
than likely a smell caused by human
activity. Suddenly as if out of fresh air,
they were confronted by a fearsome
looking character. He stood and stared at
them from the far side of the clearing,
muttering in a strange dialect. Then he
pointed to JT and indicated that he should
follow him into the jungle.

"Ye canna go in there alone after
him Boss, it may be a trap".

JT realised who these people were
and announced he would follow the
fearsome character.

"Jock, you look after the patrol and be on standby for any distress signal. If you hear my whistle, then come running. They probably want some of our gear for a trouble-free passage".

After struggling for several minutes through the dense undergrowth, JT emerged into a large clearing. There was a shambolic hut to one side and a smaller dilapidated shed alongside. Several other constructions were strewn around the place like gazebos. At the far end of the clearing, there was a long single-storey building made from local woods, bamboo, and an assortment of handmade bricks. It looked like a temporary forest farm 'Longhouse' which housed several families. A wide range of pots, pans, containers, and wood-burning stoves littering the scene. He had seen more modern versions of these types of buildings in less remote areas, but this was an older more mysterious jungle-dwelling. JT was invited to sit on the steps, at the centre entrance to the building and told to wait.

Glancing into the gloomy interior he saw several animal skulls, knives, machetes, and other paraphernalia hanging from the interior walls. A short time later a squat tribal elder appeared at the entrance. He indicated JT should join a group of old wizened men who sat inside the entrance to the building. After a short debate amongst themselves, they announced that the group had permitted the patrol to move within their territory. This was (of course) subject to conditions; a gift to the longhouse as a show of appreciation was required. Along with a promise that the patrol would not kill any animals in the nearby forest. JT also agreed to give them compo-rations, chocolate, boiled sweets, two jungle knives and a pair of green jungle boots, so everyone was happy.

JT was then invited onto the veranda that ran the length of the building. Several small, frond covered entrances to family rooms, were strung along one side of the veranda. Each doorway adorned with strange animal shapes. An uneasy feeling overcame JT when he noticed the occasional shrunken human head, hanging from the walls. Apparently, in some of the more remote areas, such as this, they still practised headhunting. JT had heard about it before and believed it had been eradicated in most areas, but possibly not all?

He left the encampment breathing a sigh of relief, accompanied by two old women, who were to collect the pre-arranged special gifts. It had been a successful negotiation that had avoided confrontation. This meant the patrol was able to proceed, without any problems or serious consequences. The fierce-looking character returned to the same spot as before, smiled a toothless smile, then pointed a gnarled finger as a way of telling the patrol to 'fling their hook'!

When they were alone 'The Highlander' muttered.

"My God Boss, I wouldn't like to get on the wrong side of that lot. Did you see the machete and knives that ugly weirdo carried? Besides the bloody ancient blunderbuss, he had slung over his shoulder".

"You're right Jock, these people could make life difficult for us if we upset them. Fortunately for us, they are inclined to support (British) soldiers" replied JT.

During the next few days, the patrol began to gel and work as a team. The morale was good, considering the conditions they had experienced over the past few days. Fortunately, it was the final day of a four-day jungle training exercise. So, they were all anxiously heading into the most welcomed homerun. One thing was sure, no one would ever forget the scene they were about to be confronted with!

None of the team had expected to be where they were at that moment, concealed beside the path in the shadowy fringe of dense undergrowth. They had stood in silence, witnessing a sickening scene, as the pack of feral dogs mustered on a wide section of track. Led by a large male dog, they appeared to be unaware of the patrol standing a few yards away in the shadows. Looking anxious and agitated, they stared towards the point from which they had emerged, as if waiting for late arrival. It soon became clear they had been waiting for just one individual female.

Even before she arrived, the patrol heard the unnatural sound of tin, clanking on objects and scraping along the ground. She stepped onto the track to reveal a front paw trapped in a tin can, held secure by the serrated half removed lid. The lid had forced itself into her flesh and bone, which she had been struggling to remove for a long time. Maggots oozed out of her eyes, mouth, nose, and every other orifice, as her head swung from side to side in agony. A mother dog for sure, her underbelly had several large low hanging teats, that dribbled a liquid puss on to the ground beneath her feet.

The pack circled and nudged her in a desperate effort to help her move forward. They whined encouragement and barked in frustration when she did not move another step. Then, as if by a signal the whole pack faced the direction of the patrol. Howling and snarling they charged towards the onlookers, as if in defence of the dying matriarch.

"Stand still and hold your ground. Any sign of weakness and they will tear us to pieces. Use your machetes if you have to", shouted JT.

After a short stand-off, the pack backed away to attend to their beloved sister. They surrounded her as if to protect her, but it was a sad farewell to *'the mother'*. It seemed the pack decided they could do no more for her and were asking the patrol to end her misery! With heads bowed, they followed the lead dog and disappeared into the surrounding bush.

"My God boss, we have to do something" whispered Jock.

The mother remained standing; her mouth and unseeing eyes bulged, as her head continued to swing from side to side in agonised repetition. Shuddering and shaking, she threw maggots in every direction in a desperate effort to break free. Her belly exploded, spewing out blood and masses of the 'angels of death' before she fell and lay silent in death. Rivulets had appeared on many cam-creamed faces, the hardened soldiers stood in stunned silence while listening to her dying screams of agony.

The oddest thing then happened; the whole pack reappeared, barking, and howling a lament as they circled the dead mother. Standing together they turned and stared at the patrol for several seconds as if to thank them for not interfering. With heads held high they returned in single file to the shadows under the jungle canopy, never to be seen again. As far as it concerned the mother, her suffering was over, but for most patrol members it would stay at the forefront of their memories forever. They had learned a great deal about combat skills, training, and health awareness in the difficult conditions. But they had also learned about themselves, and the importance of compassion for other living creatures.

After the caustic event, they set up an overnight camp about a hundred yards from the scene. The men worked silently, each reflecting on what had happened. JT knew the incident would affect the morale of the patrol, besides being a significant experience for each of them. In the meantime, the group had to overcome the gloom and sadness, resulting from the horrible scene they had just witnessed. Strangely, the Highlander appeared to be the most disturbed by the whole experience.

"Bloody lousy amateurs. The rotten careless stupid fools, leaving open food tins lying around with the serrated lids still attached. Stupid fools!"

JT told them he was determined to include a recommendation to the Commanding Officer; that they should make it a serious offence to leave any litter lying around in this environment. He was sure this total disregard for the environment and animal life, would incense the CO. All that remained in testament to this terrible event, was a small earth mound and an improvised cross, placed with a prayer of thanks for ending her suffering. In his report, JT attempted to describe the incident as best he could, but nothing he said had enough impact, to highlight the emotional effect on those who had witnessed it.

A job 'well done' concluded the Commanding Officers report. With the added comment:

"The British Army has always strived to be a compassionate, well-trained fighting force. You have epitomised that belief and you should be proud".

"Death is inevitable, but unimaginable suffering is far, far worse".

COMPASSION

So you think you're tough? You may look and act tough. But can you honestly say that in the above circumstances you would not be sympathetic, concerned and upset, when witnessing the demise of that unfortunate animal?

Compassion is a term used for positive emotion, expressed thoughtfully and decently. You want to help out, but circumstances prevent you from doing so! If you were involved in the above incident, would it test your mettle? Would you feel sorrow, sadness and shame, for the thoughtless acts of other human beings, who should know better?

Even JOHN WAYNE cried when he shot his badly injured horse!

FAREWELL TO
A MOTHER

I picked up my pack and dug at the ground. I Straitened my back and left a small mound. I said my farewells to new friends on that day and wished them well as they went on their way.

3

TREPIDATION

EAST AND WEST

GERMANY

THE CORRIDOR

(Germany 1970s)

The Only Way Is West!

The odd feeling, I had of apprehension quickly changed to one of dread. Should I slow down? should I speed up? Should I stop? or should I carry on driving along the potholed East Germany autobahn towards my destination? This was my first drive along the highway, known as 'The Corridor', between West Germany and West Berlin. To get to this point, I had been interviewed, interrogated, and subjected to the most horrendously steep learning curve. Now, being confronted by a serious situation was alarming, to say the least.

It is essential that I broadly outline the political and geographical situation. Before the end of the second world war, a huge European country existed known as Germany. At the end of WW11, the country was divided into East Germany and West Germany. The West is controlled and developed by the Western alliance of nations. The East was suppressed by a communist regime that did not believe in development.

The former German capital city of Berlin was almost centrally located in East Germany. Because of its strategic value, it was divided into Eastern and Western sectors of administration. As a result, Berlin became a divided city, with terrible consequences for people within the region. The Western sectors were primarily controlled and developed by Britain, France, and America. The Eastern sector was controlled and left underdeveloped, under the complete and absolute domination of the 'United Soviet States of Russia'.

The city became a melting pot of intrigue and savage suppression, behind the infamous 'Berlin Wall'. The separation of communities and families caused many deaths, through efforts to reunite friends and families. Escape attempts of dissidents from the Eastern sector to the

West caused tremendous loss of life. The Eastern sector was sealed behind the 'Wall', with very secure and limited access or entry points called 'Checkpoints'. Infringement of the oppressive Russian rule, or attempts to escape usually resulted in death, or many deaths. Evidence of this can be found in historical museum displays and records, particularly the one at 'Checkpoint Charlie'. Which was the major gateway, to and from, the Eastern and Western sectors?

Now, here I was alone in the Eastern sector, travelling through enemy territory. An alien world with many hazards, such as the two military vehicles following me. One, an East German jeep type vehicle, the other a Russian personnel carrier. It was all I could do, to stay calm and do exactly as I had been told by the American military police a short time earlier. Easier said than done, I thought, as the two vehicles moved closer and closer to my rear bumper. *'Gulags'* sprung to mind, as I contemplated what should be done in this situation.

For several years, the political circumstances fluctuated greatly between East and West. Action and reaction within the corridor could change dramatically, often with dire consequences for travellers. As expected, an increase in volatility could lead to incarceration in some remote East German establishment. Or even worse, a Gulag, somewhere in the frozen wilderness of Siberia!

I had approached the Allied checkpoint with the usual British aplomb and confidence. After 200 miles of beautifully smooth easy driving, along the West German Autobahn. The comfortable drive had rendered me impervious to stress. I began to enjoy the new adventure I had been instructed to embark upon. I looked forward to traversing the 'dark side!' The journey through West Germany took me through pleasant scenery. Passing many well maintained attractively painted small towns and villages. It remained the same right up to the Allied checkpoint, where populated areas became less frequent and shrouded in dense colourful forests. Occasionally, one could see minor roads meandering through the trees, with rare glimpses of casual transportation.

The checkpoint at the border (Alpha) was of reasonably modern construction. Complete with restaurant, rest-rooms and loads of well-dressed military and civilian officials. On arrival, I was instructed to report to the military administration office and told to wait for an interview. While I was there, I had the opportunity to read some of the many warning signs on walls, posts, and windows. All were in several languages, mainly English, German, French and Russian.

This impressing upon me the importance and seriousness of the journey I was about to undertake. After a while, a very stern-looking gentleman and an American Senior Officer waved me to a seat opposite. I had the distinct feeling that I was being assessed for my capability to embark on such a journey (which later proved to be the case).

The interview was extremely detailed and lasted about half an hour. Lots of do's and even more don'ts, with detailed route plans, small maps, and danger markers. If these were not followed precisely it could lead to serious consequences. Not only from East Germans or Russians but also the allied military police. By the time I exited the building I was almost a quivering wreck. However, with all the necessary papers in my possession, I walked slowly to my car to reflect upon the information and details I had been given.

My car had been checked for fuel, emergency equipment, roadworthiness, and mileage, before proceeding to the East German customs barrier. One of the conditions for Allied military personnel at that time was not to communicate or associate with East Germany police or officials, under any circumstances. This was because they were not recognised as a legitimate force by the USA/ UK and others from the Western Alliance.

At the barrier I was met by a brutally tough-looking Russian guard, there was no verbal communication, just a glare full of menace. This guy was trying to stare me to death and almost succeeded. With a wave of his hand, he directed me to the Soviet checkpoint several yards further ahead. I parked the car at the point indicated, besides what looked like a garden shed. This turned out to be the dreaded guard-post. I switched off the engine grabbed my documents and stepped out of the vehicle.

The car door had to remain open and the keys left on the dashboard. The drill had been rehearsed in detail; I was to stand to attention, face the Russian guard and salute him, even though I wore no military uniform. He responded by returning my salute and indicated I was to enter the wooden shack-like building. Not a single word was spoken, no sign of acknowledgement given, or any form of emotion by either the Russian or me. For the duration of my time in the building, I knew he would be searching for the car, inside and out.

After entering the guard post, I stood alone in the darkened interior for several minutes fearing for the worst. A small hatch opened (which I had not noticed earlier) with an almighty crash. A hand reached out on the end of a uniformed Russian arm, indicating I should deposit my documents therein. The hand snatched my documents and slammed the hatch shut, almost catching my fingers in the process. I began to realise the seriousness of this adventure into the unknown. I stood alone nervously waiting for what seemed to be hours, but it was probably about fifteen minutes.

The hatch re-opened, my papers slammed on to the shelf before the hatch closed for the last time. There had been no instruction, direction, or communication. Presumably, one had to take the initiative and leave the hut and report back to the Russian guard, which proved to be the case. Salutations were again conducted before I re-entered my car. But, in the interim I had proved one thing at least;

that Russian guards were human after all. Because the pack of American cigarettes that I had deliberately left on the driver's seat, had been replaced by a Russian cap badge!

Motoring on for about a half-mile to an East Germany border post, I handed over my newly acquired Russian pass. The barrier raised and I set off along the decomposed motorway towards Berlin. I was acutely aware that there would be a similar process when I arrived at the border crossing into the famous Olympic city of Berlin. Satisfied that I had plenty of time, to think about the rules of engagement and incident management, I relaxed and began my journey into the unknown.

The East German countryside took on a different appearance from West Germany, it was noticeably flat, tree-less, and boring. The road had deteriorated considerably, due to past decades of neglect by the East Germany authorities.

Potholes were large and frequently quite deep. Probably the cause of many incidents that would attract closer attention, by the East German or Russian military. This was a road set apart from the remainder of East Germany's population. A pathway that no other East Germans would venture near too, without fear of serious retribution. Such as detention, torture, and an extended holiday at one of the notorious Gulags, somewhere in the Soviet North.

I later learned the reason for such a dramatic change, between the beautiful wooded countryside of the West and the drab, flat, treeless East. The Eastern powers were convinced the enemy should be seen from a distance when they approached the border. Opposed to the Western logic, that thickly forested areas, with narrow roads, was a more effective defensive strategy.

As I pointed out earlier, the strict rules of engagement were not to be ignored under any circumstances. If the rules were broken it could lead to arrest, by the East German police. This could also lead to prosecution by the US or British authorities, after the event! Oddly, it was in these situations that the Russian Military were the only people one could expect any help from. Did they dislike the East German authorities even more than Western alliance soldiers?

The problem was compounded if one's car broke down or became involved in an accident. If this did happen, then an accident form would be passed to another traveller, in any direction. This would then be handed to the Allied authorities and help would be sent immediately. At some stages of the journey, the route could be confusing. One could easily take a wrong turn, ending up deep within the East German territory. Occasionally, one's car would be stopped by East Germany police (Stasi), under the pretext of speeding, to initiate communication in some way. Which of course, meant that one could be arrested and whipped off to some remote establishment for interrogation! The results of which could be catastrophic.

If memory serves me right, the speed limit was 50 mph, the journey time was between about three and four hours. If one arrived early, it meant one was exceeding the speed limit. If one did not arrive within the maximum time limit of four hours, a search party would be sent out to find you. In either case, the traveller would have to be prepared to explain why, in the greatest of detail, to avoid being charged with a serious offence.

Meanwhile, the two vehicles following my car had closed rapidly, reducing the gap to about a half-mile. I grew increasingly concerned, mentally rehearsing exactly what I should do if the situation worsened. Shortly after I came across a stationary vehicle, with the radio blasting out French music. The occupants were sitting on the side of the road, smoking, and chatting as if they were on holiday in Paris. 'God' I thought, I must warn these bloody fools, or they will soon be in serious trouble.

I stopped my vehicle and shouted at them to get into their car because the East

Germany Stasi and Russian escort were fast approaching.

The response, unbelievably, was "Viv la France, miserable Englishman"!

Along with some other amusing French vernacular! I assumed it was amusing because they all fell about laughing.

I shouted again "get in your car, now".

Before pulling away and moving on along the motorway. A short distance further along the highway, I pulled into the side of the road and looked in my rear-view mirror. As I watched, all hell broke loose as the trio was set upon by East German police. The young vulgar French woman was shouting abuse while attempting to kiss one of the East Germany policemen. All she got in return was a slap across the face and a rough entry to the military vehicle, along with her companions.

The Russians simply stood by and looked on with obvious glee. I made a mental note of where the incident occurred while pondering on the fate of the ruddy stupid French tourists? I knew they were being roughly manhandled and possibly being treated like criminals. I learned later that my moving on, was the best thing to do in the circumstances. Also, that the French group had been taken away to an unknown destination! Thank God it was not me I thought, but then realised the awful situation the daft ruddy French idiots had got themselves into. At this point, I was far away from any personal threat, so I stopped my car for a couple of minutes and made some notes, about what had happened. I would mention this to the guard Officer at the allied checkpoint (Bravo) into Berlin as soon as I arrived.

While I had been concentrating on the incident I almost turned onto the wrong motorway. Fortunately, managing to swerve in time to correct the error. A recheck of the maps and reference points confirmed I had almost taken the road to central East Germany. It is difficult to explain how it felt to be so alone, so vulnerable, and so dependent on my ability to negotiate this highway to salvation!

The remainder of the journey was uneventful and thoroughly boring, except for the interesting isolated dull villages and small towns. These places reflected the deprivation faced by local East German communities. The roads were generally constructed with gravel or dirt, very few vehicles used them other than official-looking military or police vehicles. The unpainted houses outlined in the coldest ambient environment that one can imagine. Occasionally, animals could be seen in remote fields, along with morose-looking smoke-belching factories and dull steel bridges, over even duller dark rivers. It was a constant reminder of the subdued population of this Communist governed country. A place I was glad to be passing through, and not one I wished to remain in for longer than necessary.

I arrived at the Berlin 'Bravo' checkpoint within the pre-scheduled time limit. Feeling relief and exhilaration, having successfully negotiated the Corridor for the very first time. Little did I know that my journey was quite a long way from being completed. The ruddy French group of '*silly burgers*' were due to make a positive contribution, towards a lengthy and agonising series of interviews, before I was finally allowed into the glorious city of Berlin. The incident I had witnessed involving the French car and its occupants became a major incident. The extent to which I was not fully informed. French, American, and British authorities wanted to know the details of when, where, how the incident materialised. Having repeated the circumstances several times, to several individuals and interview teams, I was finally allowed to proceed.

The view of the huge lake as I entered Berlin, was beautiful and brimming with sailing dinghies and other sporting activities. It was truly a wonderful site. I was extremely happy and longed to celebrate with a cool beer and a chaser, at the Union Jack Club hostel. I intended to carry out my work at the Olympic stadium and swimming pool during the next few days, but for now, a few hours of relaxation were essential! The following day, I decided to spend some time seeing the sites and feeling the buzz of this famous city.

All went well on all these activities, including the course at the Olympic swimming pool. I also had the opportunity to stand on the actual grass in the Olympic stadium. Pausing for thought about the spectators who had been present, when Adolf Hitler stood and witnessed the feats of the great Jessy Owens. Unfortunately, the time had come to prepare for my return journey to West Germany.

I had seen and stood on both sides of the infamous Berlin wall. I had attended the opera 'Tosca' at the world-famous East Berlin opera-house, in the Russian sector. I had seen the evidence of destruction at the remains of the landmark church.

Visited the famous Berlin Bathhouse, been roared at by huge lions and tigers at the equally famous Berlin Zoo. But the time had now come to face the return Journey, via checkpoints (friend and foe). Besides the potted miserable motorway for hundreds of kilometres. However, my prayers were answered, allowing me to have an incident-free journey back to the beautiful modern welcoming country, called West Germany.

I had the good fortune to experience this journey on several more occasions, but never quite got rid of the feeling of trepidation. Now, thankfully, there is no 'Wall' there are no 'Checkpoints' there is no East-West divide. Most notably, Berlin remains the most attractive and pleasant place to visit. A drive along the old autobahn would be the best possible way, of understanding the historic significance and beauty of this glorious city.

END

I fully appreciate why JF Kennedy uttered the famous words 'ich bin eine Berliner'.

For Friends, Brothers
and three lost French souls.

TREPIDATION

No matter who you are, or what you have achieved in life, you will always be confronted by fear and anxiety. The collywobbles feeling inside can be caused by nervousness, fear of consequences, or simply critical need.

Unrepeatable historic events, such as The Corridor' reflected in the story above, are genuinely great ways to inform or explain to our descendants. The fear of consequence, the unknown, or the possibility of failure, must be experienced at one time or another, in everyone's life!

If you have not experienced failure or the fear of it, then you have not lived!

REMINISCENCE

Life is but a moment in the earthly realm.
A path determined by who is at the helm.
What is favoured will be told

Be brave, be true, be bold.

4

INTRIGUE

SOUTH EAST ASIA

REGIONAL COUNTRIES

BRUNEI

MYANMAR (BURMA)

CAMBODIA

TIMOR-LESTE

INDONESIA

LAOS

MALAYSIA

BORNEO

PHILLIPPINES

SINGAPORE

THAILAND

VIETNAM

Note

The Island of BORNEO is divided between Indonesian Kalimantan (the larger portion) and the Malaysian states of Sabah and Sarawak. There is also a small independent nation enclave in the north called Brunei.

THE MYSTIC EAST

(Circa 1960)

Flowers from Bangkok

It was one of the most hostile environments possible, dense jungles, high mountains, and brutal terrorist groups. For Sappers of the elite 11 Independent field squadron, The Royal Engineers. It was a matter of 'in and out' of various regional countries as quickly as possible. Everyone was determined to stay safe, but the odds of surviving unscathed worsened the longer they were there. The engineering tasks were varied and carried out in many countries, some at short notice and great distances apart.

The unit was responsible for the construction of minor airfields, roads, railways, bridges. They were in constant demand throughout the whole of the South East Asian region. Numerous lesser task's such as buildings, water pipes, latrines, and other amenities were also included on the list of crucial construction programmes.

This was at a time when conflict raged throughout Indochina, namely Vietnam, Laos, Cambodia, and Malaysia. Most regional countries had major difficulties (CT's) communist terrorists. Regional hegemony between Malaysia and Indonesia and borders that separated many regional countries were facing clandestine intervention by associated terrorist groups. The Thai-Malay border and the demarcation lines in Borneo were prime examples of this form of infiltration and the spread of conflict. Most of South East Asia was in upheaval, with regional Armies fighting each other or engaged in guerrilla warfare. It was a dangerous time and place for any soldier to be, especially when it involved slogging through the unforgiving terrain.

It was made worse by having a bigoted, self-opinionated, inept officer, such as the second-in-command Major Laws, in charge of this project. A bit like rubbing salt into an open wound. The efforts of several reputable and experienced soldiers to keep their men alive, made more difficult by injustice and incompetence. A bloody idiot who would not have qualified as a Cub-Scout leader. The Major was a total liability to all who served under him; a man who later proved to be exactly what everyone thought he was, an incompetent fool!

The project in Thailand was related to a US assault on an area bordering Laos, Cambodia, and South Vietnam. The whole scheme relied on scheduled dates of readiness, timing, coordination, and secrecy. It was initiated to prevent the construction of a Communist terrorist highway, along the borders between Laos, Cambodia, and Vietnam. Which would later prove to be a major problem for the American forces?

On this operation, the squadron had to construct an airfield, with associated roads and bridges, a short distance away from the mighty Mekong River. The river bordered the countries of Laos, Thailand, Cambodia, and Vietnam. From its origins in China to the site of the new airfield, it had grown to become a huge arterial waterway. Used by large numbers of boats, Chinese junks, coastal steamers, ferries, and many other forms of water transport. Traders travelled back and forth along the powerful waterway, day, and night, with goods from as far as China and beyond. This waterway was the lifeblood of all the countries it passed, on its journey to the South China Sea.

Although the river and its associated tributaries had immense value, in terms of trade, it also had problems with piracy. Smuggling and the movement of insurgent terrorist groups was a serious hazard. This was also a conduit of serious activity by groups of terrorists, vagabonds, murderers, and the like. It was obviously of major concern to the USA, Britain and the anti-communist alliances that supported them. Regular patrols on the river paid small dividends, but they did create an opportunity to study the enemy movement of goods and manpower.

All nations along its banks had the freedom to use the waterway for legitimate reasons. So, it is not hard to imagine how easy or difficult this was, to either of the combating ideologies! As a professional soldier serving with a section of Combat Engineers, JT had subjected his men to a tough training regime for the past couple of months. Most of them were experienced combat Engineers or plant operators, but a few were fresh out of the UK and hopelessly green. Even so, they had to be ready for anything after a short period of acclimatisation and training.

They would inevitably face injury or death; if not from CT's (Communist Terrorists) and bandits, then from animals, reptiles, or the stultifying hot and humid environment. As section leader, JT was determined to keep them alive in this dangerous part of the world. If casualties occurred, then they would evacuate them quickly. However, it was abundantly clear, that it would be extremely hard to evacuate from the jungle, or the drought-ridden, dusty paddy fields.

Before setting off for Thailand the team received a briefing about the hazards they could face. Particular attention was given to a North Vietnamese guerrilla leader by the name of General VO NGUYEN GIAP, who was responsible for the construction of the highway (secretive trail) along the Lao-Vietnamese border. It was designed to enable his forces easy access into South Vietnam. There were also obvious dangers from various known terrorist groups in the region, such as the Viet Cong (Vietnamese) Khmer Rouge (Cambodia) and Pathet Lao (Laos) led by a cruel and sadistic leader known as 'TA MOK'.

A week later the section moved to Thailand where the conditions were even more primitive than expected. The drought-ridden Paddy fields had turned into dust bowls with the consistency of talcum powder, which made engineering work especially difficult. There was some relief when the team discovered several hastily constructed houses, built on platforms alongside the primitive access road. Further inquiries revealed that these houses contained an oasis of bars, fashionably occupied by beautiful ladies from Ubon and Bangkok.

At this time, JT's additional duties included, the role of health officer for the squadron. As such he became responsible for preventing the spread of diseases, particularly ones of a sexual nature. This duty required him to keep a record of the results of the women's blood tests. To watch out for any signs of infection. All the girls were friendly and cooperated with the blood test regime. But they made it clear that JT would not have access to any of them!

As time passed JT began to think he had some sort of affliction, but it soon became obvious that he had been reserved for Anna 'The Madam'. Anna was a knowledgeable, sophisticated woman who brought him flowers whenever she returned from her regular trips to Ubon and Bangkok. He was flattered, but as a traditional Brit, he was wary and kept his distance. There was a possibility that Anna could be in league with local CT's. It was also disconcerting, being the only soldier in the whole encampment who had sweet-scented flowers alongside his bunk. This became a source of mild embarrassment, because of the nature of the 'squaddie'. Especially in such dusty, arid, featureless surroundings.

A short few weeks later the was peace was abruptly shattered, upon the arrival of his nemesis Major Laws. Elevated to Officer Commanding the project, Laws quickly ruined everything the construction team has achieved during the first few weeks. He imposed pointless rules and regulations that had a disastrous effect on the whole project. JT had struggled to pacify the men, telling them he would confront the Major if it was justified.

During the following weeks, the Major became friendly with the local 'Big Cheese'. A Chinese/Thai businessman and local government official. 'Li Big Cheese' was a smirking, slimy character, who drank Jack Daniels whisky like water. He also smoked sweet-scented American cigarettes, that masked his foul body odour. The plump over-indulged individual had control over a large area of land containing several 'Borrow Pits'. These pits were vital for extracting Laterite, a valuable mineral needed to strengthen the road and airfield runway surfaces. 'Li Big Cheese' also had a hold over the beautiful Madam Anna and the other girls, through the threat of death to their families. Most of whom lived in Laos, Thailand, or Cambodia. Forced to pass on information about the project, Anna and the girls fed 'Old Hat' information to their tormentor, to avoid any repercussions. Anna was a well-educated woman, who loved art and traditional dance, she was not happy being a spy! Preferring the company of British troops, much more than the sinister group of people that otherwise controlled her life.

A constant struggle soon developed between plant engineers and local landowners. As the access to the pits became almost impossible. This had the effect of delaying the project, which in turn allowed 'Li Big Cheese' to receive special treatment, and regular entry into the confines of the officer's mess. Often done at the behest of the cow-towing Major Laws, during dedicated events or celebrations. This gave the Chinese businessman many opportunities to secret information, for his friends the Viet Cong. Whose sole intention was to delay or destroy the airfield project altogether. Intelligence sources had recently confirmed that CT activity had increased along the borders between Laos-Cambodia and Vietnam. There were obvious signs of more violent and regular attacks on construction sites. It became clear that information was filtering through to the CT's, about security and progress at the airfield and other related sites.

At that time, the Major must have thought 'Li Big Cheese' influenced high places, he refused to acknowledge the Chinaman was anything other than a friend to the project. Ever since Major Laws had arrived, he made a life for the team miserable, which had disastrous effects on morale and production. This resulted in several accidents and minor casualties. The men grew increasingly uneasy as the project moved into its critical stage. Especially since drought had turned the muddy, rice paddy fields, into a dust bowl.

Enveloped in a thick fog of 'Bull Dust' the plant operators worked in almost blind conditions. The choked machines making it impossible to work efficiently, or effectively. Eventually, things took a turn for the worst when Laws refused to suspend the project, to await the arrival of special protective equipment. This led to a confrontation between JT and the Major, who then threatened to remove JT from the project. Shortly after, a young plant engineer was severely injured while operating machinery at the sight. A haze of Bull Dust resulted in a caterpillar tractor ploughing into machinery, the young engineer would never walk again.

JT made it clear to the Major he would present his report to Colonel McClure when he returned to Malaya. The enraged Laws shouted abuse at JT (overheard by several team members) before telling him he would face disciplinary action and charges of insubordination. JT knew that a healthy workforce would achieve better and timelier results. He also suspected that Colonel McClure (the CO) realized that Laws was a self-proclaimed egotistical snob. Who liked hobnobbing with the elite, in the futile hope of gaining prestigious appointments? However, JT knew he had to tread carefully when he approached his Commanding Officer.

Meantime, American President John F Kennedy made an announcement, that he would increase levels of military aid to South Vietnam. As a result, attacks on the Thai project became much more serious, involving greater numbers of CT's and munitions. There was a much greater determination by General VO NGUYEN GIAP, the North Vietnamese guerrilla warfare leader, to destroy the project. The alliance between the Viet Cong, Khmer Rouge and Lao Communists, became increasingly vocal. This resulted in the deaths of thousands of innocent people across the region. Locally, it was about to get worse, under the cruel leadership of 'TA MOOK'. The vicious Lao butcher would stop at nothing, to kill as many British and American troops as possible.

CT terror tactics successfully subdued regional villages, who faced torture and mutilation. Their bodies often displayed in prominent places, as a warning not to associate with any organization opposed to them. It was clear that the CT had gained access to confidential information, about arrival dates of plant and equipment, trial landings of planes, troop movement and security arrangements at the site.

'Li Big Cheese' was known to visit the houses on stilts, from time to time, to place himself in Madam Anna's office. The signs were always there; a partially consumed bottle of Jack Daniels whisky, the strong smell of sweet-scented American cigarettes and the distinctively foul body odour. As far as JT was concerned, it was clear that the Chinese businessman had a powerful hold over Madam Anna and the girls.

At the first opportunity, JT asked Anna, why the businessman had such control over them. She told him that 'Li Big Cheese' owned the houses, controlled the business. He regularly threatened her and the girl's families with torture or death, if they disobeyed his orders. It did not matter where in South East Asia they came from, or where their families lived. His evil tentacles would search them out and they would be killed without mercy. Over the following few weeks, JT became more amenable to Anna. Their relationship developed into an intimate liaison. Laws found out about the new friendship, accusing JT of repetitive misconduct and collusion. Taking great pleasure confining him to camp.

The men were now feeling mutinous towards Laws. Due to his obnoxious stupidity and abuse, he made them look increasingly incompetent. Team morale was low, and work began to fall behind schedule. Delays caused by machine failures and breathing problems affected the project. It began to look as though it would not be completed in time, for the arrival of the first scheduled US transit aircraft and troops.

Because of deteriorating conditions, Laws became more and more agitated, his treatment of the troops became more abusive and intolerable. It was then that the team reminded JT of the 'tethering hooks' on Snake Island, in Singapore. Suggesting that they too were prisoners, not specialist British Sappers. At every opportunity Major Laws became more vociferous, accusing JT of encouraging a rebellious attitude within the troop. The Major told him he faced removal from the site and serious disciplinary charges.

As the seriousness of the situation became unbearable, JT reflected on the years he has worked to be the best. He tried to contain himself in the face of such animosity, reminding himself that he had one great advantage. He was one of only a few to have served alongside special forces, which afforded him a great deal of respect from senior officers. Subsequently, special branch officers interviewed JT and his team, to answer accusations of collusion. Proving otherwise was not easy, because of the Major's rank and powerful position. JT began to feel like a cornered rat; cornered rats fight ferociously for survival!

Meanwhile, Colonel McClure was becoming increasingly concerned about reports from Major Laws. The Colonel has worked with JT on many occasions over the past few years, but began to wonder if the first-class section commander was losing his self-control! McClure had no reason to believe the Major was being anything other than efficient and honest. He decided to sort this out quickly, to be ready for the scheduled, big joint US/UK operation. The first wave of US helicopters and transport aircraft were due to arrive in a couple of weeks.

Over the next few days, JT kept his head down but managed to see Anna from time to time. One evening she confronted him hysterically. She was inconsolable after discovering that a Laotian terrorist group had killed her whole family. She knew this was her punishment from 'li Big Cheese' because of her failure to fully cooperate with him. She also wanted to protect JT from the horrible Major Laws and 'Li Big Cheese', so she had decided on a path of revenge. She informed the investigating officers of CT compounds in the nearby jungle and of 'Li Big Cheese's' connections to them.

There was then an attempt to rid the area of these terrorist groups. JT was tasked to take his section, along with other infantry patrols, to look for the CT strongholds. They later discovered two encampments which had signs of very recent occupation. But it looked as though the residents had received some warning! Two hours later, after searching the surrounding jungle, they came across a large group of CT's and a firefight ensued. This resulted in the deaths of several insurgents and a British infantryman. A Malay soldier fell to his death in a terrible CT pit trap, which had a dramatic effect on the rest of the Malay contingent. This was bad, but at least it was not anyone amongst the men who JT had sworn to protect.

Shortly after the medical evacuation of the injured, they moved back to the collection of buildings. During an intensive search, they find clues to who these people were. Chinese ration packs, explosives, ammunition, and radio equipment. Further searching led to the discovery of documents, proving that a link existed between the airfield construction site and regional insurgent groups.

The most significant find was a table with partly eaten meals, along with a large bottle of Jack Daniels whisky and an open pack of strongly scented American cigarettes. JT became incensed, swearing he would sort out 'Li Big Cheese' as soon as he arrived back at the airfield site. 'Li Big Cheese's' betrayal was, without doubt, a career-ending embarrassment for Laws. Especially, since he had attended many functions in Ubon and Bangkok, as a special guest of the treacherous Thai/Chinese businessman. 'Li Big Cheese' subsequently disappeared and the Major was returned to Malaya pending an investigation.

JT was absolved of all charges and returned to the construction work. with renewed determination. The airstrip project began again in earnest. Time had been lost, but with Laws gone the team worked together and rallied to make the deadline. Instead of finding a replacement for Laws, Colonel McClure decided to oversee the project himself. Immediately implementing a positive 'Hearts and minds' strategy with the locals. The Colonel decided to make the unorthodox decision, to join in with JT's team as part of the hearts and mind programme. One significant action was to locate a Tiger, that had killed and half-eaten, several villagers over the past few months. Eventually, with the help of indigenous trackers, they located and killed the beast.

The invisible wall of subterfuge had finally been removed, information about dissident groups began to flood in. Security at the project improved, attacks by insurgents became less frequent and less effective. JT and Anna's friendship developed into a meaningful relationship. Things moved along smoothly until Anna's sudden disappearance. He searched for her for several days, until information came in that she was a captive at a CT encampment somewhere in Cambodia. After several weeks of further futile searching by infantry patrols, they discovered she had been killed. JT was devastated by the news and knew 'Li Big Cheese' had got his evil revenge. He hoped treacherous sod suffers and rots in hell.

Towards the end of the project, JT had news about 'Li Big Cheese'. Who had been found, hanging in bits, from several trees outside a remote Lao village? Nobody was sure whether he had been killed by insurgents or by local tribesmen, but JT knew that Anna had got her payback. Henceforth, the terrorist attacks on vulnerable villagers became less frequent, they were at last, able to smile and cut the rubber trees. With the villager's spitting contemptuously at the remains of the evil 'Li Big Cheese', each time they left and returned to their village.

Before returning to Malaya the body of his beloved Anna had been returned to Thailand. She was given a traditional Buddhist burial, on the outskirts of Ubon.

On his posting back to the UK, JT got to learn about the fate of Major Laws, who had been given a job of Recruitment Officer at some remote outpost in Scotland.

It later transpired he was dishonourably discharged from the service, the details of which have never been revealed. 'Forgive and forget'. Never! Never! Never!

JT continued his career, serving in several other parts of the world before his retirement. He often looks back with a mixture of pride, joy and sadness. During the Thai experience, not a single member of his team was lost. The men responsible for such soul-destroying experiences, for him and his comrades, had been brought to justice. Albeit in a horrible way, about which he could not feel the slightest sympathy. Most vividly, because of great sadness, over the loss of his beautiful Anna in such terrible circumstances.

Since his retirement, JT has travelled to Ubon and placed flowers on Anna's grave. But none could ever match the beauty, or the heady scent, of the wonderful 'Flowers from Bangkok'.

END

JUNGLE

Blood on legs and ankles

The hungry leeches were gone

I will not forget this shrouded place

The memory will live on.

SNAKE ISLAND

'Snake Island' is a small island on the outer fringes of Singapore harbour. Once used as a prison for POW'S, during the occupation of Singapore by the Japanese forces. Infested with deadly snakes, spiders, scorpions and rats, the island would have been hell on earth for all the poor souls held there. The 'tethering hooks' referred to in the above story, had been used to suspend prisoners as a form of punishment or torture.

"Old soldiers never die; they simply fade away!"

INTRIGUE

Aren't people stimulated by an element of intrigue in their lives? The secrets, the plot's, the mystery of entanglement and curious interest that draws a person into an adventure.

The above story will have been a catalyst, for those of us who have probed the realms of intrigue. To pick up the pen and write about their own, exciting adventures and experiences. For sure, we all have a hidden desire for mystery, intrigue, and adventure. Tap into your exotic memories and tell us all about them if you dare!

5

ERUDITION

(Indonesia)

KOMODO DRAGON

This creature is the size of a large crocodile
and just as dangerous.

VARANUS
KOMODOENSIS

(KOMODO DRAGON)
Unexpected?

The island of Komodo lays within the Lower Sunda islands, in the Indonesian archipelago. The island is surrounded by turbulent seas and treacherous currents. This is where the Indian Ocean meets the Pacific Ocean! Massive whirlpools are a common sight when approaching the island. The topography is volcanic with high cliffs, rugged mountains and shoreline made up of dull darkish muddy sandbanks.

When setting foot on the island it becomes clear, that this remote place is relatively new to outsiders and tourism. Beyond the beaches, it has wide areas of scrubland and dry forest, which is easily negotiated by well-trodden footpaths. Areas alongside these footpaths are relatively clear of bushes and scrub, which act as safety zones. Beyond these zones, the forest becomes denser, more tangled and threatening. Venturing into these areas would be unwise without the protection of local guides.

The forest and scrubland eventually give way to higher grassy slopes and trees, until it takes on a more mountainous almost alpine appearance. Both temperature and Humidity play a large part in any planning process, especially when trekking and fallowing the signals from transmitters. These transmitters are attached to previously captured dragons, who could travel many miles hunting for prey. This animal can stay in the same spot for days, waiting for some unfortunate victim to wander too close.

With speeds up to 25 miles an hour and huge strength, they can nip out of hiding and bite the unlucky victim. If they failed to bring the victim down, they would follow it, often for days, until it inevitably collapsed with gangrene from the venomous bite. It then consumed the animal as quickly as possible before other dragons joined in the feast. It is a gruesome sight, watching these huge lizards' squabble over what had been a Buffalo or Deer a few minutes earlier. They are renowned for being extremely noisy and messy eaters?

Our scientific team were all excited at the prospect of seeing more of these dangerous monitor lizards. We had spent the previous ten days hunting, capturing, and examining the legendary Komodo dragons, on the larger island of Flores. However, the island of the same name 'Komodo' was their most natural home ground. As such it was the best place to find and see them in any number. Islanders had been given bad advice, which made them believe they would benefit financially from exploitation. The short-term goals, designed to attract tourists to this mysterious island, was extraordinarily successful. But as a sustainable programme, it was seriously flawed.

These lizards can kill and devour a fully-grown Buffalo in a single sitting. But their main prey species, are the mid-sized Deer and wild Pig, that inhabit the island. From time to time, they have been known to dispense with unsuspecting human beings. Some being snatched from their beds or caught wandered carelessly on the beaches, or in the surrounding area. It was interesting to see, how the local human population were able to avoid confrontation with these animals. There seemed to be mutual respect, a

"you keep out of my way and I'll keep out of your way", attitude.

It was also noticeable that most villagers carried a stout long stick as a form of defence. The dragons had an intense dislike for strikes to the snout. Which was one hypothesis I did not want to test out!

Currently, there are thought to be less than 6.000 in existence, over a small range of Indonesian islands, mainly Komodo and Flores. They are known to be excellent swimmers and are occasionally seen swimming far out at sea. Often finding homes on smaller nearby islands, such as Rinca, Gili Montag and Gili Dasami, all of which lay within the Komodo National Park. The Komodo Dragon is very heavily built, with a powerful crocodilian sinuousness and appetite. It has tough scaly skin that looks like old armour plate and claws that can dismember large prey in seconds. The snake-like tongue flicks in and out, constantly testing the surrounding air. While at the same time leaving a residue of poisonous saliva, containing as much as 50 strains of bacteria, dangling from its jaws. The shark-like teeth shred the prey to death and great chunks are swallowed as quickly as possible. Dragons do not like to share! They are cold-blooded animals that thrive in hot temperatures, actively hunting during the day. Staying cool in burrows when it gets too hot, which also become warmer safe havens at night.

These huge lizards are mainly solitary animals, that can vary in colour from dark blues and greens, through to a murky grey. Some have been found at least 10 feet in length and weighing over 200 Lbs. They can consume 80% of their body weight in one sitting and have superb vision. Being able to spot prey from great distances, they slowly manoeuvre themselves into an attacking position. There is no doubt why these lizards were referred to as Dragons by ancient mariners, who first came across them sometime in the late 19th century. One strange fact that has recently come to light, is that the female animal is parthenogenic, which means they can produce offspring without sexual contact. Consequently, the isolation of one female on a small remote rocky island is not necessarily the end!

The team of scientists came from a range of sciences, including animal habitation, and health, husbandry and human transmigration, social anthropology and environmental science, tourism. The team were responsible for researching and evaluating factors, which would influence the lives of the Komodo Dragons. Besides the effect on the local human population. As part of the programme, it was essential to study the effect that tourism had on the animals, as well as on the indigenous human population. It was also necessary to study the prey species of the dragons, such as Deer, Wild Pig and Water Buffalo. For millennia, the animal had relied upon the prey species for survival. But it was now evident that the animals were becoming lazy and unhealthy. With fewer prey species being hunted by the dragons, the number of wild Pigs and Deer began to escalate to unmanageable proportions on the island.

The research was conducted, to determine how it was possible to avoid the extinction, of this isolated group of giant lizards. At the same time, it would try to help the indigenous population benefit from a sustainable, natural, and unique resource. There was plenty of evidence to suggest that tourism was solely responsible for the declining health of the Komodo dragons. Furthermore, it was clear that the present arrangements and strategies were not sustainable in the long-term.

By increasing the numbers of tourists to the island, the authorities had hoped to provide a profitable income source. To facilitate this process, they made it easier for the once allusive creatures to be seen on demand. This was done by introducing a system of live baiting, where tethered goats were used as live bait. These so-called meals were arranged to coincide with the arrival times of tourist groups. Large ocean liners carried hundreds of tourists to the island, to be assembled at viewing galleries in specified areas. This would enable them time to witness a terrifying and most gruesome spectacle. When dragons mutilated and consuming the terrified goats. This practice was a very unpleasant experience for many tourists, but it did mean that they were able to see, first-hand, the monster lizard at work.

Over time the practice led to a deterioration in the health of the dragons, who became lazy and lethargic. As a result, they became less inclined to hunt for themselves. The Dragon's reproduction process was in serious jeopardy and began to decline. The practice of tethering was frowned upon by animal rights groups and subsequently stopped. It was the objective of this scientific team to research and make recommendations regarding any alternative sustainable options. Several key issues had to be considered, including the animals' health and their declining numbers. This had to be achieved whilst retaining a valuable source of income for local people. Through the development of a lucrative and sustainable tourism programme.

Thus, a programme was arranged to gather scientists from around the world. All had a range of high-level skills, which would be used conjunctively to affect change in the approach to tourism on the island. There were three team members from the USA, one of which was an extremely intelligent and interesting Blackfoot Indian. Both his compatriots were also very lively and greatly increased the enjoyment of the programme. Another, a remarkably interesting Japanese deep-sea diver, with oceanographic expertise, who continuously took samples on land and in the surrounding seas?

To complement the group, we had four from the UK, two Australians, three Indonesians and a Malaysian. Bringing a wide range of skills together to achieve the best possible outcome. The aim of which, would lead to the implementation of an alternative sustainable tourist strategy. One that could be used for the benefit of the indigenous population. The team began its programme, on the western tip of the larger Indonesian island of Flores.

This beautiful island was used to gather more information about these animals. From a primitive base camp out in the wilderness, it was a daily strenuous trek, to find and assess some of these rare animals. The campsite was within striking distance of a Manggari village, where they made us feel very welcome. During our stay we were honoured to observe a range of dance and fighting skills, to entertain us.

During the first few weeks, several animals were captured in locally made traps. They were then measured, weighed, gender-determined and tagged with satellite fixtures across their hindquarters. This was a risky operation, especially when some dragons were three meters or more in length and weighing in at hundreds of pounds. Fortunately, local rangers were always close by, offering support and advice. On several occasions, this proved to be especially useful indeed. Occasionally when animals were released from traps they would immediately turn and run at their captors, who swiftly climbed the nearest trees to safety.

There are few animals scarier than angry Komodo Dragons! Strange as it may seem, team members were only doing what juvenile Dragons would do to avoid being eaten by their species. As youngsters, the dragons would spend most of their time hunting insects, snakes, and other unfortunate treetop dwellers. Only when they became big enough to outrun their larger cousin's, would they dare to venture down to the ground?

After a couple of weeks in total isolation, the team were finally about to see a lot more of our elusive quarry. The move to Komodo island was arranged because the population of dragons was far greater and much more accessible. Due to the goat tethering strategy, which we were unanimously opposed to.

Moving to Komodo island by small boat, was an experience that many will not forget in a hurry. The boat was just about the length of three large cars. It had wooden seating along its gunwales, that often sank perilously close to the water's surface. It did not take much imagination to feel a little vulnerable from time to time. The route across a turbulent sea, from Flores to Komodo, lasted about five hours. At the halfway stage we manage to stop at a small islet which had a clean white sandy beach. A light picnic was arranged, but a swim of about fifty yards was necessary to get there from the boat. It was a pleasant stay but on our return to the boat, we very nearly lost one of our team to the sea. Over the past hour, the sea became increasingly turbulent. Fortunately, a rescue mission was successfully launched. Everyone clapped and laughed with relief and joy when it was successfully over. Apart from the few insect bites, stings, and fearful screams, this was the only truly dangerous situation we experienced.

Moving on, we passed small lesser islands and huge partially submerged rocks with sheer sides. At one point it became necessary to circumnavigate a huge whirlpool, seething and steaming ferociously. We all prayed the small craft with the 'Put-Put' engine would not falter! Safely past the dreadful hazard, we relaxed and enjoyed the magnificent outline of Komodo island. We were all fascinated as it grew from a speck on the horizon, into what looked like the mysterious island out of 'Jurassic Park'. The dark sandy shoreline, broken up by areas of mangrove forest and the occasional cluster of human dwellings on stilts.

The interior of the island was dominated by high sparsely wooded mountains, that added to its mystical appeal. The accommodation was a modern wooden construction designed to fulfil the needs of the many foreign visitors. A small museum and historical library, along with the inevitable gift shop, were set within an amenity building at the edge of the forest. Surprisingly, it was not unusual to see the occasional Komodo dragon, wandering around beneath the wooden platforms of the accommodation blocks.

We heard that a few months earlier a young local man had been attacked by a Dragon, while he was having an afternoon siesta. The huge animal had climbed the steps of his house, walked along the veranda, and entered the living quarters. The young man was lying asleep on his reed mattress when the animal grabbed him by his leg and dragged him out to the veranda. It was fortunate, for him, that the remainder of the family were resting nearby and quickly went to the rescue. They used their long sticks, prodding the dragon until it dropped its victim before it beat a hasty retreat.

A helicopter was sent from Flores to take the gravely injured man to the general hospital. The chap was extremely lucky to live because the infection from these bites is highly venomous and usually leads to death. Several months later the victim had recovered sufficiently to leave the hospital, but with only one leg.

On the first morning of field research on Komodo, we followed our guide along the dry forest and mountain trails. We had been walking for an hour when our

Manggari tracker unexpectedly stopped. He turned to the group and began to apologise profusely, about some incident that happened in London a week earlier. Initially, we could not determine what he was talking about? His English was extremely limited. as was our grasp of Manggari. A combined Indonesian, English, French and Japanese, was eventually used to make sense of it all.

Showing his concern so dramatically, was his way of expressing his, and his peoples' sorrow, over something we knew nothing about. With genuine sincerity, he tearfully tried to explain about the event, which had happened while we were isolated in field research conditions. He must have realised the team had not heard of the incident when he got no reaction to his earlier comment about the sad event.

This led to the revelation, that struck members of the team like a thunderbolt! They were horrified to hear of the dreadful news, of 'the death of the beloved Princess Dianna' in a road accident. At first, we all stood back in disbelief, looking intently at the distraught guide.

The most significant and dramatic moment came, when the guide highlighted the reaction to her death, on the streets of London. The streets had been lined with millions of beautiful flowers. According to the guide, the wonderful Princess had recently visited this region and spoken to his people. It was certainly a moving and traumatic experience for the team. Until then they had been working, studying, and researching in an atmosphere of adventure, camaraderie and peace.

This event did not detract from the purpose of the research, but sobriety did move to a prominent position in the programme. The reaction to the news was dramatic and universally upsetting. Each member was aware of the contribution the Princess had made to conservation and peace, in many areas of the world. To the benefit of millions of people. Due to the upsetting nature of the news, the day's research was cancelled. This was not the only bad news for the team, a few days later we heard that 'Mother Teresa' had also died. For some time after, there was a sort of disbelief at these extremely sad events. Particularly as some team members had been involved, as associates, with either one or in some cases, even both, globally loved individuals. Sad, sad, sad.

Several days later, many tasks had been satisfactorily completed. The team made the perilous journey back to the island of Flores. All wishing they were aboard one of the gigantic tourism ships, rather than the fragile little craft with the 'Put-Putt' engine. On arrival we assembled in comfort, within the beautiful beach accommodation, to say our farewells. It had been an exciting, interesting adventure and a worthwhile scientific experience. Most importantly it had been a period of bonding, a programme almost eclipsed by an unexpected turn of events. Which only served to strengthen the links between us. Now, more than two decades later, there are signs that the Earth-Watch initiative had positive results.

Improvements have been made on sustainable strategies, which have resulted in an increasingly healthy population of Komodo Dragons. The dragon population is increasing in numbers and health. The prey species, which had been spiralling out of control, now regulated by natural processes. Finally, the indigenous human population can look forward, with greater confidence, to a sustainable tourism resource. The research is ongoing, there are teams continuously monitoring the situation.

Overall, a successful, positive, and worth-while research and development programme. The whole of which, was designed to protect the species from extinction, whilst providing a sustainable income for local inhabitants. The only downside was the unfortunate, untimely, and tragic news of the deaths of the internationally respected and loved, Diana Princess of Wales and the death of Mother Teresa.

END

TO FRIENDS AND COLLEAGUES ON
THE MILLENNIUM FELLOWSHIP
PROGRAMME.

ERUDITION

A meaningful term used for individuals who are prepared to study and learn, through a combination of theoretical and practical field research. Individuals who have a pragmatic approach to education, which is possibly the most rewarding activity one can embark upon. The difference between knowing and not knowing is dependent on circumstances and choice. As we learn, we become aware of our limitations, that there is so much more we do not know or understand.

My personal choice is wide, and I find most subjects interesting. But I, do what most of us do, select the topics that interest me most, then do my best to understand them as fully as possible.

I wish I had the time to do more!

TIME

Humans cast long shadows
As they move along in time
Responsibility and conservation
While enjoying life is fine.

6

DEVOTION

(Courage)

MATERNAL LOVE

The image was drawn by Rachael Roberts

A LESSON IN COURAGE
(CIRCA 2006)

CHICKEN?

I had spent over 30 years in the British Army, sometimes in difficult dangerous circumstances. I knew a great deal, or so I thought, about fear and courage. The experiences and adventures I had over the years, as an individual and as part of a team, gave me what I felt was an in-depth appreciation of what was meant by courage. Two decades later my understanding of the concept of courage was severely tested. The following story is about my moment of true enlightenment. At that moment I was caught unprepared, for the effect it would have on me; the so-called, brave, tough, and experienced soldier.

My wife, the dog and I (in order of seniority) made it a regular feature of our summer holidays, to travel in our old VW camper van. Even so, we loved to discover new and exciting destinations. We did not have to travel great distances, because our home is in East Yorkshire. With easy access to the Derbyshire Peaks National Park, the North Yorkshire Moors, the Yorkshire Wolds, and the Lake District. Only a couple of hours away from the great countryside, so we could enjoy these areas without the hassle of long periods on motorways.

We most regularly toured the North Yorkshire Moore's and the Yorkshire Wolds. Often packing our camper van at a moment's notice. This happened at least a half dozen times a year; it was as if a great big cloud was being removed from above our heads. The forested areas of Crompton, Dalby, and the moorland, were a blessed relief from the humdrum of work and drudgery of City Life. The present eight-day trip had been wonderful and the weather favourable. Our love and appreciation of nature had grown exponentially, after stays at incredible locations throughout the region. Eventually, we began to feel a little tired and weary, after so many days of travel and excitement. Now, it was time to go home for a well-earned rest!

Our camper van moved smoothly along the narrow roads of the North Yorkshire Moor, between the resort of Whitby and the village of Rosedale. The evening was drawing in as we reached a very steep hill. Caution was an essential consideration, before beginning our descent down the winding, narrow-wooded lane. We prayed the brakes on our vintage VW camper van would hold, during the twisting long descent to the picturesque village a mile or so below. If they failed, we would certainly have had serious problems bringing the old van safely to a stop. I decided I would head for the banks of the road and hope for the best if this became a problem. The grade was 1 in 7 as I recall, but thankfully the weather was pleasant, sunny, and dry. So, it was not unreasonable to believe, that by gently brushing the bank-side in a very low gear, it would eventually enable us to stop.

'Old faithful' had not let us down during the past few days of wandering across moorland, dale, and beautiful Yorkshire countryside. There had been one or two false starts and a few minor hiccups at certain points. But overall, our faithful camper van had proved herself to be a reliable friend. Although we had confidence in our transport, there was a feeling of apprehension at the prospect before us. This was going to be a huge test for our van and me as the driver. Which, if successfully negotiated, would lead to the most satisfying and exciting final leg of our wonderful holiday?

At the bottom of the hill, the village lay quaint and inviting. It was a great place to stop and rest, before the final 30-mile drive home. On arrival at the village, we would enjoy the usual cream scones and tea, or ice-cream at one of the 'olde-worlde'

shops in the village square. Rosedale Abbey would tower above the square, but even that would look tiny in the backdrop of the hills beyond. It is a village packed with interesting features in idyllic surroundings. A place where one can rest and appreciate country-life and nature, in an atmosphere of peace and tranquillity.

We began our descent by crossing the roadside cattle grills, designed to prevent cattle or sheep leaving the relative safety of moorland. The rattling sound emanating from the iron rollers as we crossed, acted as a reminder of the hazardous drive down the steepest hill we had yet encountered. Having achieved what we had set out to do, which was to enjoy the remoteness and beauty of the countryside. As far away as possible from the drudgery and monotony of modernity.

However, we did not underestimate the difficulties we could encounter in this beautiful, but at times hazardous, environment. Deep in concentration at the task that lay ahead, we manoeuvred carefully around the first bend in the narrow road. A few cautious minutes later, we encountered an object in the middle of the road. It appeared to be a large colourful dead bird, lying in a flattened heap, with wings spread wide apart. There were a few brief moments of sorrow for the 'roadkill' before we attempted to stop the old camper van. It soon became apparent we would not be able to stop in time to avoid compounding the problem, by squashing the poor animal even further.

Thinking of a last resort action, I considered driving the van into the tree-lined bank. This also proved to be an impossible strategy, because of the sheer bankside, along with the narrow steep road. We were determined to slow down as much as possible, without burning the brake pads and leaving ourselves in terrible danger. Gingerly passing over the spread-eagled bird, we realised it was a large chicken. More than likely, it had been run over by another vehicle. We had seen a few careless, thoughtless idiots in too much of a hurry, during our holiday.

A few yards further along we came to a farmyard gateway, which allowed us to pull in and stop the van. Meanwhile, the incident had removed our fear of the hill, replacing it with sadness and concern for the innocent creature. Sitting in silence, we looked in our rear-view mirrors, to see if we had avoided causing the poor creature greater humility. Which, would have been an even more poignant reminder of the tragedy of death, even in chickens?

It was then that we had the incredible revelation, of what love and family meant. Of true courage in the face of almost insurmountable odds. Like a phoenix rising, the bundle of colourful feathers stood up and spread her wings. She shook her feathers and proudly clucked, as several fluffy yellow bundles emerged from beneath her bosom.

A feeling of intense relief and sheer joy replaced our sadness, like a warm blanket of downy feathers. The whole event was magical, especially when we saw the hen lead her brood towards the safety of the hedgerow. The experience was a reminder of the actions and reactions, of many of my military colleagues when under fire. Heads down, look insignificant, maintain a low profile, and stay focused. Whilst at the same time prepare to use the weapons and equipment at our disposal.

But this was different! The hen had nothing but her fragile frame and colourful feathers, with which to defend herself and her clutch of beautiful chicks. She could have abandoned them and saved herself quite easily, by running to the hedgerow on her own. As everyone knows, chickens can run at an extremely fast pace and would be able to get out from under, comfortably! The chickens' decision to risk her own life to protect her family was an extraordinary display of courage. Especially, as it was from such an insignificant source (according to most people) as a chicken?

I have no idea from where the common phrase 'cowardly as a chicken' originated, or how it came into being. But due to this experience, I can categorically say there is absolutely nothing cowardly about them. The bravery displayed by this chicken proved, it is one analogy that could not be further from the truth. Those few moments will be etched in my memory until the day I die. Yet, there was even more enchantment to come from a most unusual source.

As we refocused on the road ahead, we noticed a large cockerel strutting up the road towards the hen. The colourful, supremely handsome fellow reminded me of an Aztec king. Dressed in the finest robes of vivid red, green, and gold that shimmered in the fading light. All topped off with a high crown of the brightest, deepest maroon, that moved in rhythm to his positive steps of superiority. He headed towards the beleaguered hen, as if to offer his support, whilst still looking angry and full of concern for his family.

As he passed our position, he stood up tall and flapped his huge wings, then made the loudest cockerel call I had ever heard. I was sure he winked at me, as he strutted like a Guards Officer towards his family. Before firmly ushering them to the safety of a nearby farmyard.

We resumed our dangerous journey down the steep hill, still in awe at what we had just witnessed. Driving in silence until we arrived at the village below. Our utter weariness had disappeared, leaving us feeling refreshed and elated. By an experience that had left us temporarily speechless. Our holiday was made so much more memorable by the experience, one we would never forget. We had witnessed, a most wonderful and enchanting display of bravery and devotion. Supported by the unfettered unflinching support of the 'other half'!

During my life, I have witnessed many tragic accidents, seen death and terrible injuries. I had looked with admiration upon those who had displayed courage and conviction. With scorn and contempt upon displays of 'man's inhumanity to man'. I am now more aware of the value of life, in all its forms. Of the courage, it takes to fulfil it with dignity. As time passes, we often talk about the 'Brave Hen', 'The Devoted Cockerel' and their family. Moreover, about the important lesson, we had learned about courage, even in chickens.

END

TRAVELLING

Travel through time and space
Find new and exciting destinations
Have many joyful experiences
And much more with imagination.

COURAGE

Courage is a strange mixture of in-built forces, which determines whether we 'Do or whether we 'Do not. It takes the form of action, in a wide range of circumstances, from offensive to defensive. Fighting on the battlefront or performing dangerous pursuits, are examples.

Overcoming fear of failure is like delivering care to people who have infectious diseases, or a severe personality disorder. Climbing Everest is no greater test of courage, than an Arachnophobe holding a great big hairy spider. What can be more courageous than staring death in the face, to save your family? Chickens are normally thought to lack courage, hence the term 'You're a Chicken'.

After the above incident, I developed much healthier respect for Chickens.

7
FEAR

THE EMERALD ISLE

THE HOME FRONT

(N.I. The 1970s)

FACING DEATH?

It is not in a person's interest to 'blow one's own trumpet', or to claim to be brave and heroic. So, before I begin this tale, I should like to point out that I am neither a hero nor a musician! As is often the case, we find ourselves in situations that require 'flight or fight' reactions. In the case of soldiers, the individual coping mechanism is easier to control. Decisions to make a stand, or to run, become clearer and more clinical. In military service, it is the training that leads to a greater appreciation of danger. Especially, in situations that can have dire consequences, for the individual or the group.

Faith plays a large part in military service, faith in oneself, faith in comrades and faith in what we are supposed to be doing. There is, of course, religious faith, which is a matter for the individual. Witnessing too many tragic and horrible situations may have a bearing upon what one believed in the past and what one believes because of such experiences.

Why? Is probably the most important and prolific question that has ever been solicited. Upon consideration, it is reasonably easy to understand and to appreciate. Ask me if I believe in God and I will tell you, that on some occasions I cried out for his help. Even though I had some doubt about his existence. I can only assume, that due to my upbringing and religious education it became an integral part of my persona. This belief was much more influential and defined during childhood. Especially when measured against an adult with major life experiences.

How can so many terrible events take place? What drives people to elicit pain, suffering and degradation upon others? Why? What does it achieve? I understand that everyone is unique and each of us has aims, aspirations and characteristics of our own. Some may feel justified in retaliation and rightly so, others may turn the other cheek! But some seek to justify cause and hope to make the right decision.

With that little, but a candid introduction, I will tell you a tale about the time I served as a soldier in Northern Ireland. A time when I learned a great deal about human nature, compassion and most definitely about fear. As well as the occasional enjoyment of 'the amber nectar' (Guinness) most of the people I met were friendly, welcoming, and certainly volatile. The countryside is beautiful, but the towns and cities, at that time, were full of antibodies, mine in particular!

At that time, the region was embroiled in the terrible conflict, between one faction and another. It was difficult to decide who was right and who was wrong, or even to determine if there was a right or a wrong? But that was not the purpose of our visit. All we were expected to do, was to attempt to maintain peace by keeping the factions apart. Our other main role was to protect innocent bystanders if there were any? Some areas are definitely 'no go' areas but had to be patrolled regularly, for one reason or another. I often wondered why I was moving along dark deserted streets, dashing from cover to cover, praying the moon did not appear from behind a cloud.

Constant feelings of utter futility were overwhelming, especially when the sound of 'drums' emanated from darkened street corners and terraced houses. The 'drums' were a mixture of signals, being passed between streets and between homes. An integral system devised to keep tabs on the whereabouts of military patrols.

Patrol members were acutely aware of being closely monitored; each hoped the ambuscade would never materialise. These signals were made up of rattling dustbin lids, penny whistles, screaming babies (slapped to make them cry) and loud Irish music. But, most discerning of all, was the rattle of roof tiles and movements silhouetted against the night sky. These were anxious moments that could change instantly, to life-threatening confrontation. These situations could inexorably lead to injury or death of a comrade, or comrades!

Getting back to the safety of the improvised headquarters, was a blessed relief. Although it always entailed tedious but necessary safety checks, before being rewarded with a hot brew and a meal. A stand down and rest from one's exertions, often interrupted by another emergency call-out. Not once, but sometimes several times. Sleep was a luxury that few enjoyed for more than a couple of hours at a time if one was lucky. Those improvised cardboard boxes once used as bedrooms, in large commandeered rooms, were soon to become welcomed cocoons. These were made even more beautiful, by photographs of friends and families, along with the occasional pin-up!

During the initial period of our visit to the province, we talked a great deal about current events. The adrenaline-pumping situation was a common theme, but it soon became a 'no-no' after someone had been hurt or killed. Many soldiers became dependent on adrenalin stimulation, some looked forward to difficult encounters. This had the effect of coping with sleep deprivation and life in the fast lane! Most people know that in these situations, deep sleep is virtually impossible.

This sort of 'less is more, more is less' situation soon led to internal strife, which consequently led to mistakes in unloading bays. Some of these mistakes were serious, some fatal. But it all added to the tension and trauma, that is known as active service. There is nothing quite so traumatic and soul-destroying, as having one of 'your own' killed. Whether it be by a bullet, bomb or through an unfortunate accident. Being witness to many of the terrible results and consequences, of murderous enemy attacks can be soul-destroying. As time dragged on, from day's into week's and week's into months, stress and lack of sleep influenced health and more importantly, moral.

At one point the unit had a particularly hazardous week of serious incidents. This involved shootings in communities, shooting at troops on patrol, the bombing of houses and vehicles. Riots were frequent and deaths of civilians, police and military had suddenly escalated. Patrols were intensified because observation posts were constantly under attack. For all the old sweats, who served there at that time, several areas instilled a feeling of dread and foreboding. The Markets, a large complex council housing estate, alongside the River Lagan. A damp cold and dismal place, full of characters intent on making it as uncomfortable and dangerous as possible; for those who were stupid enough or compelled to venture into the area.

Divis Flats was another such place, at the junction of Falls Road and Shankill road. A large complex of council flats, within and adjoining one of the tallest tower blocks in Belfast. During the 1970s the top two floors of the tower block became an observation post for the British army. At the height of the troubles, the only way to get up there was by helicopter. These areas were extremely dangerous places, where patrols were constantly under threat of attack. As a result, there were many casualties and deaths of soldiers and civilians. Many other unsafe areas existed, but it would take a whole book to describe or discuss them all. I will leave out some of these electrifying places of horror and murder, from this short tale.

Two days of extreme violence in the city centre led to an incident that I shall always find truly fascinating, yet faith destroying! The event made me wonder if I belonged to humanity. I was completely taken aback by the sinister subtle evil, coming from an unexpected source. While on a routine patrol around the side roads of central Belfast, we approached a long line of women queueing outside a fish and chip shop. The wonderful smells of fresh frying wafted along on the breeze, leaving us with a lust for some goodies therein. We were not able to stop, but we relaxed, thinking of what it would be like to have some of the tasty cuisines.

This was the first and last time we ever made the mistake of relaxing, whilst on patrol! As we passed the queue on the opposite side of the narrow road, the merry housewives started to make it clear what they thought of us. I learned more swear-words and inflammatory abusive language in that short period than I thought possible. Colourful comments were hurled at the patrol, about personal legitimacy, their families and loved ones. Soul destroying abuse and terrible language, from the mouths of (what we expected to be) helpless women and mothers. As trained soldiers, we were hardened to abuse and resisted the temptation to 'kick-ass'.

Unfortunately, on this occasion we were distracted and failed to notice many of the women moving to cut off 'tail-end Charlie'. The end man of the patrol had been forced into a doorway, completely separated from the remainder of the patrol, by a throng of wildcat murderous women.

It was certainly a pre-meditated event, evident by the knives, machetes, and other weaponry they carried with them. It was not often, that patrol members were ordered to cock their weapons, or to prepare to release safety catches. But on this occasion, it was essential. The result was an immediate dispersal of the riotous group of women. Only then, was the patrol able to rescue the trapped soldier, who in that noticeably short, period had sustained several serious injuries. Made worse, by the fact that the seemingly innocent queue of women, was just like any other queue outside a fish shop, anywhere in the UK. It was a revelation and a lesson in active service mentality, which led to updated skills and training strategies.

There were many incidents that I could mention, but one was the ultimate test of personal mettle. A rapid 'call-out' to a huge city centre explosion, led us to a scene of absolute carnage. On arrival, the team was made responsible for cordoning off the surrounding area. As the team leader, I had to position the team, to ensure the protection of all the emergency services involved. Every major incident attracted teams from a variety of organisations, including Fire, Ambulance,

Bomb disposal, Media, and Military. It was not uncommon for response teams to be targeted by additional pre-determined attacks. Many of which could be even more destructive than the original incident. As first responders, it was one's responsibility to assess the situation and to take appropriate action.

On this occasion, the initial ring of protection and security was established. All that remained to do, was to conduct an on-site visual inspection. Once this had been completed, it would be the responsibility of the incoming Military Police and specialist teams to take the lead.

At this incident, I witnessed scenes that made even the strongest team members baulk and curse uncontrollably. The first was the site of a car that had been destroyed by the explosion. Bits of the car was spread over a wide area but contained within a small market square. Most of the surrounding windows had been blown out, and glass lay everywhere. In the centre of the square, one of the car doors lay on the ground, inside uppermost; with something resembling steam coming from its surface. Closer inspection revealed a horrific sight; a human leg devoid of clothing or footwear lay on the door, with steaming entrails attached, spilling out onto the surrounding pavers.

It is difficult to describe the sights and smells associated with this type of incident. The discolouration of bodies, the burned-out car, the steaming remains of charred bodies and caramelised blood. The smell of petrol, mixed with toxic fumes from explosives, served to make it more horrible. Blood-soaked pavements and surrounding walls added to the mix, making the scene a detritus laden quagmire of broken glass, twisted metal, and human remains. Further, inspection revealed that two persons had been present in the car during the explosion. Those occupants were headed towards some pre-determined target. But they had either primed the bomb incorrectly or ran out of time. Even so, the feeling of revulsion and horror at the resulting chaos, was as it would have been for any person or persons involved.

Unfortunately, the worst was yet to come, a body was discovered in one of the adjacent shop doorways. It appeared to be a female in a sitting position, who had been blown into the doorway. No clothing, no hair, or any markings other than what we assumed to be breasts. On closer inspection, it became clear that the persons' legs were missing. The lower part of the body had been blown upwards with such force that it, initially, appeared to be a female. Other factors proved it was not!

It was a time of deep reflection about life's purpose, family, and humanity. Days later we were informed that the head of one of the occupants of the car, had, at last, been found. The circumstances of which, must have been exceptionally traumatic for the third-floor office staff of a nearby building.

The typing pool ladies had witnessed a flock of seagulls, pecking at an object on the ledge outside their office window; that object needs no introduction!

The purpose of reviewing some of these horrific incidents is to set the scene, in what can only be described as a dangerous and frightening place to be. I did mention earlier in this tale 'belief in God' So you may now be able to decide, whether circumstances played a large part in belief or not?

It all began after the events of the terrible month's referred to above. The pressure on the task force had to be countered, by measures that would alleviate pent-up emotions. This would reduce the risks of internal accidents, as well as minimising rebellious attitudes in tired frustrated troops. Mini sporting events: such as quizzes and competitions were organised. A range of meaningful rewards was made available for winners, in the form of extra day's leave on repatriation or occasional monitory incentive. Arrangements were made for soccer and rugby teams to play other teams, both military and civilian, inside safety zones.

Sports clubs in the region were asked to participate in indoor games: such as squash, darts, dominoes, and a multitude of other social activities. This plan was not without its problems, security and maintenance of duty rosters were an obvious consideration. I happened to be a reasonably competent squash player and a member of the regimental team. We all welcomed the opportunity to put our skills against reputable opposition, whilst at the same time having a social break from tedium and stress. It was subsequently arranged for the squash team to visit a well-known club in a relatively safe area. The club was on the opposite bank of the Lagan River from the dreaded Markets.

Everything was meticulously planned for the special evening's entertainment, and safe passage to and from our headquarters. Which happened to be located on the same side of the river as the Markets. The five-man team were delivered to the venue by the land rover at about seven-thirty, arrangements made for pickup at 11 pm. The evening was a huge success and enjoyed by visitors and hosts alike. The time for pick up past, while we anxiously waited a further hour for the minibus to arrive. We were informed that there was an emergency, which had created a shortage of vehicles and personnel. As a result, we had to use a patrol vehicle to return to base. Four of the team were able to squeeze into the patrol vehicle, alongside the patrol team itself. But the fifth member could not get in and extremely dangerous. The fifth member happened to be me!

As I had to ensure the men arrived back at base as quickly as possible. I accepted the offer of a lift to the bridge, by my new Irish friends! What I did not realise was that it would only be to this side of the bridge?

They would not dare cross it themselves for fear of going into enemy territory (Markets).

Meanwhile, the patrol land-rover, which had promised to pick me up at the bridge, assumed it would be on the side nearest to the headquarters. The dilemma was, they were waiting for me at one end and I was waiting for them at the other! Patrol vehicles do not want to be stationary for too long, so they continued circling the area and hoped I would soon appear. At the other end of the bridge, I began to worry that they were not able to pick me up. I began to feel a little nervous and was almost overcome by a sense of foreboding. My mind began to play games with my invincibility, as the butterflies danced to a terrible tune in my stomach. What if they failed to turn up at all? What was I going to do? When should I move to get back to base?

The hardest thing to do in these circumstances was to control one's fears and think rationally. After what seemed to be a lifetime, I managed to suppress my panic. Then decided to make my way across the bridge, to get back to base somehow. It was a critical fact and my duty, to get back to my base as quickly as possible. Besides, it had occurred to me that the promise of my delivery to the bridge may not have been interpreted correctly. As was often the case with our Irish friends. Eventual I concluded that the patrol might have expected me to arrive at the other end of the bridge.

The bridge was several hundred yards in length, it may have been shorter or longer, but it was a considerable distance as far as I was concerned. I eventually decided to walk along the bridge, slowly and casually to avoid attracting unwelcome attention. Carrying my squash racket, I would increase my pace, as I approached the other end of the longest bridge ever built! If I were targeted, I would have little or no chance of getting away. It was a clear night, visibility was good, the weather calm and there was not a single vehicle or person to be seen.

About halfway across, I noticed an old ramshackle car pull out from under the far side of the bridge. It had come from the markets area. The car made its way slowly along the bridge towards me, passing at a measured pace. I began to get that same feeling as I had earlier. A churning stomach and sickening awareness, that makes its presence felt, whenever one realises that danger was imminent. Forcing myself to remain as calm as possible, under the circumstances, I began to think of the scarce variety of options open to me.

"These thugs must not get me, if they do, I am a goner".

The trembling seemed to subside slightly before the flight factor took over.

I had noticed that there were at least two occupants in the car. They stared at this strange character walking along the bridge, with a squash racket, late at night. To this day I believe they must have thought, this cannot be possible, it was all too simple. Nobody in their right mind would do such a thing! Fortunately for me, caution must have got the better of them, so they drove on towards the point from which I had started my walk. I felt a great sense of relief and carried on my merry way, hoping I would soon be picked up by one of the patrols. During this time, the whole world appeared to be silent. Until the silence was suddenly broken by the screeching of car tyres, as the car made a rapid turn at the end of the bridge. As it moved back towards my position, I knew I was in serious trouble. I looked desperately for a way out, but there were few options.

Option one, was to wait until the car stopped and the occupants got out. Then make a run for the end of the bridge, at twice the speed of the Olympic sprint record. The second option was to wait until the car stopped and the occupants approached me, so I could bash them with my squash racket? Neither of these options seemed a particularly sound idea! But I had one more option, which was to leap off the bridge into the river and attempt to swim to the nearest bank. I happened to be a strong swimmer, but unfortunately, the bloody tide was out. I looked down at the river below, only to see mini rivulets trickling through thick slimy, mud, glistening and moist from the recent tidal outflow. A thirty-foot drop, mud possibly fifteen to twenty feet thick and a man of twelve stone descending at speed, was not compatible!

By this time, the car was edging closer, and I felt extremely vulnerable.

"Christ' I shouted to myself, for God's sake think of something or start running and hope for the best".

So many things passed through my mind. I knew I was hopelessly trapped in a situation, where it would be better to fight than to be bustled into that car? They would not shoot me, because they would rather extract possible information by horrible forms of interrogation. I knew what had happened to other soldiers when they had been caught by these characters, it was not a pleasant thought.

"God help me" I mumbled, as I began to run towards the end of the bridge at least a couple of hundred yards away.

Just as the incident was about to come to a terrible conclusion, I saw and heard the patrol land-rover come screaming on to the bridge. With lights blazing and horns blowing, it sped towards me at a hell of a speed. The threatening old car suddenly speeded up, shot past me and them, then disappeared into the darkness of the Markets. Grabbed by the scruff of the neck, I was unceremoniously pulled into the back of the Land Rover. I honestly cannot remember the journey back to base, but I learned a great deal during that incident. Never go it alone, never rely on friendly natives for help, most importantly pray.

I believe it was a strange coincidence that my rescuers arrived, just in the nick of time. I often have nightmares about the incident, almost half a century later. The question of whether I believe in God has been answered, even though I still find it difficult to understand. Please believe me when I tell you, that in desperate life-threatening situations, where all hope is lost, you will call for his help, as I did.

END

LACHRYMOSE SOULS

Lachrymose souls beseeching call.

Yearning to escape the fall

Plea to Deity to hear ones voice

Keeping the faith is our best choice.

FEAR

Fear manifests itself when people are confronted by harm or death. Often, fear can be controlled by who one is with at the time. There being greater forces involved, such as honour, love, and teamwork. These forces can momentarily override the immediate threat, which lessens the initial impact and allows more time to think! To show no fear is a superficial quality, that some individuals possess in abundance. But, when all is said and done, nobody is fearless. However, the more one is exposed to a threat, the better one can cope with fear.

"Courage my friends, you are not alone. For those who say, 'No Fear' are surely fear prone!"

8

BELONGING

CROSSING THAT BRIDGE!

Photograph by kind permission of Author
Karl Jackson.

'HARRY'S GAME'
"First of the few"

ISBN 9781916265103

RITE OF PASSAGE
(LIFETIME)

PRIVILEGE AND HONOUR

Without doubt, talking about oneself at any length would be onerous and monotonous in the extreme. So, I have decided to take a more judicious approach to the topic of 'Rite of Passage'. There are many, who claim membership to a range of organisations. Others may have had, as I have had, a wide range of experiences. Whether it be in sport, military service, or education. Almost all of us can lay claim to recognition of special achievement, which earns membership of an organisation or group.

What is unacceptable, is for a person to claim this rite through false representation, or by exaggerated achievement and lying? False claims are inevitably revealed over time, particularly when it comes to University Degrees, Medals for Bravery, Honours and Awards or membership of special organisations.

Often, such claims range from belonging to outfits like The Royal Marine Commandos, The SBS, The SAS, The PARA's, or The Royal Army Physical Training Corps'. Or claims of fictitious medical qualifications, to name just a few examples. It is easy for one to understand why false claims are made; humans are, after all, motivated by greed, status, and self-importance. Albeit, mostly based upon a false premise which allows them to gain financially, socially, or historically. On the other hand, for all those who have genuinely earned that 'Rite', it is a source of immense pride, satisfaction, and honour.

In this account, I offer my personal view of what I believe to be 'My Rite of Passage', into an organisation of which I am extremely proud. I am immensely privileged to have developed lifelong associations and close friendships, during and after membership. I also believe that each person who has made their life worthy of note, can and should, be able to claim this rite. This is often possible in more than one enterprise, affiliation, or conquest. It is for the individual to decide if their interpretation of success is valid, whether it contributes to their quality of life and endeavours.

What is good for one person is not necessarily good for another. This can be exemplified by, the opposing views of the combat soldier and conscientious objector. One cannot and should not impose their views on others, who are different in nature and belief. While some human beings are outwardly strong and rugged, others appear to be weak and fragile. Even so, there is always some important quality concealed within, which, as we all know, can often manifest itself in advantageous ways. Suffice it to say, I know of many, who have appeared to lead less-exciting lives than myself. But! they have, at the same time, made outstanding contributions to society and the world at large.

We should not allow ourselves to be too concerned with the achievements of others while dwelling on the 'what might or could have been'. This misconception could lead some people into the realms of false prophets, or towards illicit claims of associated achievement.

From the social anthropologist viewpoint, some have had considerably more interesting and exciting experiences than others. One has personal achievements are especially important to them, so 'Up Yours' is not an acceptable attitude. Which means I consider the achievements of colleagues and friends to be exceptional. From the time I was able to walk and participate in sport, I wanted to achieve great things. This motivation became an integral part of my life, both as a soldier and as a civilian. As I grew older and wiser, I began to realise that muscle and brawn were becoming less important to me.

It became clear that more intense and determined use of intellectual ability was often necessary to achieve success. This may be the aim of some individuals, but it is not for all. However, most people aspire to belong to organisations that require intense pre-requisite examination, In one form or another. The more difficult the process of assessment, the more pride will manifest itself when one achieves the objective.

In my case, I had to complete the exceptionally difficult and tough courses, to enable my transition and acceptance into 'The Army Physical Training Corps'. Then, and only then, could I claim undisputed membership of the Corps. It was a long and strenuous journey from disabled boyhood (first story, Inspiration) to the point of admittance into this elite Corps. Nobody will ever be prouder of that achievement than I.

The Corps that I am referring to has, without doubt, contributed greatly to the health and wellbeing of the British Army. It has also proved to have been an effective and important factor in civil society. Besides contributing greatly to the armed forces of numerous other nations around the world. The effects can be measured in several ways, Military Fitness, Health, Sport, Rehabilitation, Special Forces, Education, Welfare and National Security.

Individual Corpsmen and Women can be stationed as specialist instructors, in regiments throughout the army. They can be seconded to other services like the Royal Navy, the Royal Air Force, both at home and abroad. Some are posted as advisors to other countries throughout the world, including the Far East, the Middle East, and the Americas. Teams of instructors are used to establish schools of physical recreational and adventurous training, in strategic locations around the Globe. Serving with Gurkhas, SAS, PARA's, SBS and other specialist regiments (During peacetime or on active service). This could be in any environment, anywhere in the world, including jungles, deserts, mountains, or islands. Many have been killed in World Wars, or at bridgeheads in Europe, Middle East, Africa, and Asia.

They have taken pride of place in other wars since that time; including the Malay-Indonesian confrontation in Borneo, The Korean War, The Gulf Wars, The Falkland War, and the Indian Mutiny, to name just a few. Each one acting as an individual, but integral, part of the Regiment or Unit that they have been seconded too.

The Corpsmen and Corps women could find themselves on street patrols in urban areas or as part of jungle warfare platoons. They could serve in mountain rescue, high- altitude warfare and even be seconded to Senior Officers protection teams. Some may be responsible for training army recruits at command centres. Or training officer cadets at training colleges, such as Sandhurst. They also do fantastic work as remedial therapists in military hospitals and remedial centres, in war zones throughout the world.

The Corps were and still are, responsible for the 'Fit to Fight' programme, designed to do precisely what it 'says on the tin'. Training and professionalism, as expected, are exceptionally high as one can appreciate from the above outlines.

My personal experiences as a Corpsman ranged from serving at a School of Physical Training: An Artillery Regiment: A Signal Regiment: The Royal Engineers: A Command Headquarters: The Brigade of Guards: and Training Regiments. And, on more than one occasion on active service in locations such as Northern Ireland, Europe, the Middle East, and the Far East. The experience gained was extensive as one can imagine, ranging in environments from deserts, mountains, islands, and jungles, both in peacetime and on active service.

This, compared to some individuals, is a mediocre career timeline. But each and all Corpsmen and women would and could, be expected to perform tasks at any location, in any circumstances. So, in many cases, it was the luck of the draw, or a skill factor, that determined where one ended up. My background as a Plant and Combat Engineer was a contributory factor in my career path within this elite organisation.

For readers interested in additional information about 'The Royal Army Physical Training Corps' there is an excellent website, which can be trawled for research. The Corps also has an excellent well-presented illustrated history book, which can be obtained from The Army School of Physical Training in Aldershot. A place where all Corps members lost oodles of sweat, blood and tears, for many months to achieve their goals.

END

FOX

FOX GYM WILL HAVE A SPECIAL
PLACE, IN THE HEARTS AND
MEMORIES OF CORPS MEMBERS.
FOREVER!

SUMMIT OF MOUNT SNOWDON WALES

MENS SANA IN COPORE SANO
(A healthy mind in a healthy body)

THAT'S LIFE!

'WICKED'

Whatever I do and wherever I go, I try to be civil, I also try to enjoy lots of fun and laughter. If I were Irish, I would probably write a comical poem about an Englishman. If I were English, I would probably write one about a Welshman. If I were Scottish, I probably could not write one! By heck, I am asking for trouble saying that! Joking aside, I have met and made great friends with many Irish, Welsh, Scottish and even Englishmen, during my years of military service. I have the utmost respect and regard for them and admire their different qualities.

I have put my life on the line for them on several occasions, as they have for this humble Welsh 'Son of a Gun'.

END

AUTHORS PROFILE

Born in 1939 he grew up in a small coal-mining community in South Wales called Penyrhydin, not far from the *Black Mountains*. As a child, he had to wear callipers *(toe to thigh)* until the age of 7. He enlisted in the British Army in 1954 as a boy soldier with the Royal Engineers. Trained as a combat engineer and plant operator. In 1964 he transferred into The Army Physical Training Corps.

He spent 8 years with the Royal Engineers and served in South East Asia. He spent time in deployment in the jungles of Malaya, Borneo, Thailand, Laos. He then served as a physical and adventure training specialist with the Grenadier Guards, Royal Artillery, Royal Signals & HQ BAOR (British Army of the Rhine). The future deployment included the UK, Northern Ireland, Singapore, Germany, Thailand, Borneo, and other regions of the world.

His awards include a unique Commendation (Meritorious Service) from the Air Marshall Far East Land Forces, the

Queens Silver Jubilee Medal in recognition of his work in South East Asia and BAOR.

10 years after leaving the army John decided to embark on a new adventure, into higher education at Hull University. He went on to gain a BA (Hons) degree in Asian Studies and Language (Malay, Indonesia) and an (MSc) Master's degree in Applied Social Research (Social Anthropology). He was also fortunate enough to spend 1 year at the University of Malaysia in Kuala Lumpur.

John has written and published award-winning poems and produced four books on poetry and short stories. He has also published a romantic and adventurous novel about a British soldier. Now retired, John lives with his lovely wife Jane and their faithful Labrador Harvey, in the village of Preston, Hull, East Yorkshire.

Jane and John Roberts

2011

Author's note

I am not convinced of the intrinsic value of these tales; it may well depend on whether readers are young or more mature. Even so, I thought it worth remembering and reflecting on things past, if only for the sake of historical information. Certain events and experiences depend on the situation prevailing at the time, many can no longer be experienced by anyone. I acknowledge, that there are a great number of the older generation and military veterans who have had similar experiences.

With regards and respect

JT

Royal Engineers

(Once a Sapper always a Sapper)

APPRECIATION

I wish to thank my friend Paul Obernay for his observations, and critique of my work during this publication. His advice and commentary have been invaluable and very much appreciated.

Also

Mr Karl Jackson author. For his help and advice when I needed it most.

MY UNIVERSE

In my universe I am supreme, I have choices

I am accountable, I know what lays within

I can make decisions, good or bad.

I can give or I can take, I can include

or I can exclude, or accept rapacity
I can love, or I can hate.

I can laugh or I can cry, I can walk or crawl

I can pray or be agnostic

I can be prominent or dwell in obscurity.

I can bathe in sunlight or drown in darkness

I can learn, or remain ignorant

I can exercise or remain indolent.

I can choose to help others or be egocentric

I can be weak, or I can be strong

I have absolute power.

BUT ONLY IN MY UNIVERSE!

THE FUTURE

Another book in the series of short stories will be produced, subject to the response and success of this presentation.

READERS

I would welcome any contact regarding your reflections and stories. There is (for me) greater satisfaction and pleasure, in reading factual and genuine tales of adventure and life.

OTHER WORKS BY THIS AUTHOR

THE QUARRY OF DREAMS

A pictorial library of photographs, short stories, and poetry.

ISBN: 978-1-4567-7788-3 B/W.

ISBN:978-1-4567-7530-8 Colour.

THE ENCHANTED HIGHWAY

Dedicated to poetry

ISBN: 9781478308935

THE TRANQUIL MAN

The adventures of a British soldier in the jungles of South East Asia and the urban jungles of Europe

Historic—Enlightening

Entertaining

ISBN: 9781497461543

<u>NAUGHT BUT THOUGHT</u>

Poetry and verse. Taking time out to sit and think. Everyone should do this!

ISBN: 9781787196087

All the above books are available on Amazon in hardback and eBook formats.

MESSAGE TO

MY READERS

This book is a collection of events that occurred in my life. In which I attempt to capture and reflect on the emotions, that everyone experiences at one time or another. I hope that it is accepted by readers as it is intended, unpatronizing or egocentric.

The stories are all based on true events, which I felt were worthy of inclusion in this publication. I aimed to prove that one can overcome adversity (whatever that form takes) and go on to live a full and adventurous life. There are restrictions on each of us, but what is important is to make the most of what you have.

Our aspirations and dreams often manifest themselves because of physical or mental hardship. Each one of us, from whatever background or any part of the world, can follow their dreams and contribute to human existence. Otherwise, what is the point of us being here?

I want each and everyone to feel as though they are as important as anyone else. We, my friends, are utterly unique and equally as special.

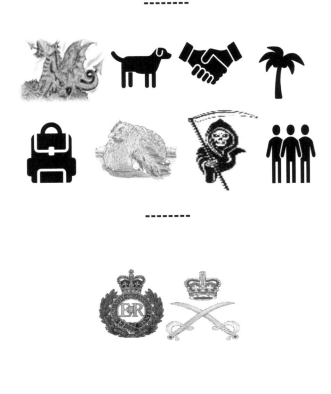

NOTES

Printed in Great Britain
by Amazon